A Student-Veteran's EXPERIENCE

with

Higher Education: The Musical Support

Enjoy my journey!!

May you find solace in your music

Dr.B.

By Dr. Peter J. Burke, EdD.
SGT, USA, Retired

A Student-Veteran's Experience with Higher Education - An Academic Journey: Prominence Publishing; www.prominencepublishing.com

A Student-Veteran's Experience with Higher Education: Social, Family, and Fraternal Support...and Peppi, too! – Burke R & W Services (e-book); https://www.linkedin.com/in/drpeterburke/

Prominence Publishing (paperback); www.prominencepublishing.com

Editing by Burke R & W Services

A Student-Veteran's Experience with Higher Education: The Musical Support / Dr. Peter J. Burke, EdD. -- 1st ed.

ISBN: 978-1-990830-75-4

Table of Contents

List of Pictures and Figures

Thanks and Dedication

Thanks to my father, Thomas P. Burke, EMCS (SSN), USN, Ret., for his love and for being the first scholar in my life; this work is also dedicated to his memory.

With thanks to my mother, Mary Burke, for her love and support during my entire academic journey, from my first words, pre-school, elementary school, junior high school, high school, and during my adult life taking classes when time (deployments) permitted, and into my doctorate. Mom did not live to say it, so she now says in heaven, "My son, the doctor!"

I want to dedicate this work to Mr. Richard Dumas, my junior high school band teacher. He kept me motivated and believed in my musical abilities. We later became good friends as adults. Thanks for everything, Mr. D!

I would also like to dedicate this work to all veterans, student-veterans, and those who experience PTSD incidents. I hope you may find at least a sense of comfort or peace in your music.

About the Author

Peter J. Burke retired from the US Army in 1996 and began his academic journey at Cameron University in 1997. He holds a BM in Horn Performance and an MA in Teaching- Secondary Vocal Music. He later earned an MMEd in Instrumental Conducting from the University of Oklahoma and his EdD in Educational Leadership in Higher Education at North Central University.

Peter J. Burke lives in Clarksville, Tennessee, and is a freelance researcher, author, educator, and veteran advocate. He is a member of ASCAP, Student Veterans of America, and is a Life Member of Kappa Kappa Psi.

Chapter 1

My Background

I'll provide context for those who have not read my first book about my academic journey. For those who have read it, please bear with me and see if you can find where I added new stuff. Read on.

I grew up as a military brat; my father was in the submarine service in the US Navy. I graduated high school and, 12 days later, reported to basic training. Upon completing basic and advanced individual training, I reported to Fort Ord, California, and the 7th Infantry Division (Light). After my time in the 7th, I was transferred to the 25th Infantry Division (Light) at Schofield Barracks, Hawai'i. I was assigned to the winter wonderland of Fort Drum, New York, and the 10th Mountain Division (Light Infantry) from warm Hawai'i. I spent my last few years in the military at Fort Sill, Oklahoma, at the Field Artillery Training Center. I retired from Fort Sill on June 30, 1996, and began my academic journey in the fall semester of 1997 at Cameron University (CU) in nearby Lawton, OK.

Picture 1:
Passport photo- 25th ID(L)

I had the honor of serving in three Light Infantry Divisions before being transferred to an artillery training base. I was in three deployable units and ended my career in a non-deployable garrison unit. Needless to say, I had quite the transition from deployable to non-deployable and then to civilian. A divorce made the first year after my retirement even more difficult. I had not only my demons from my military career but also the depression from that.

During this year, I was involved in local community music theatre activities, and with the concert band at CU, I sat in with the students and performed with their concert band. It could have been considered "auditing" that class; however, I considered it music therapy- I never filled out any paperwork to list me on the roll. I stayed musically active during this time while trying to figure out where my life was heading and what direction I wanted to go. Looking back, I can honestly say that if

I had not been active in music, my life would have been quite different, and I may have eventually become one of the 22 people per day. It was an incident in my driveway involving assault and weapons. I discussed this in my first book, which made me realize that I must get my life on a different track. The comfort and sense of self I found in music kept me on track of positive progress toward adjusting to civilian life. As a performer or conductor, I felt good on stage and felt like I had a mission. I had a purpose. Music, during my year of hell and throughout my academic journey, was one of the few constants, my faith being another, that kept me going.

Chapter 2

The Undergrad Years:
Music at Cameron University

Music, for me, continued to be a mainstay in my life. I was doing much performing, composing, and conducting, and, at times, it was a form of comfort; however, there is a difference between doing what I love, my vocation, and utilizing music to help me keep my shit together. Music helps me heal. It helps me to remember the good times and the not-so-good. Yet, despite the memories attached, some songs are painful to hear, yet we do not avoid them when we hear them. This was a common experience for me, especially with patriotic songs such as *God Bless the USA*. I'll expand on this song later.

Music at CU was motivating and inspiring, such as *Cameron Pride* or the fight song, especially at sporting events and ceremonies. Sometimes, I would think about them and remember playing or conducting them at an event when I was remembering the past. This happened often while I saw or read my memorabilia from different events. I'll talk about my fraternity's music later. Outside of that, I am sorry to say that I did not find myself finding motivation or solace in the music from CU, not for my PTSD effects. It was good school music, but that was about it. This may have been due to a severe lack of television exposure to Aggies athletics and, as a result, a lack of exposure to and familiarity with CU's music outside of that local market.

Picture 2:
Hotdog Sale at CU, 2011.

Music outside of CU at that time was a different story. My playlists were eclectic, and some had specific times when I would listen to them. I often listened to Andrew Lloyd Weber's *Phantom of the Opera* as one of those "motivational" choices, especially at home or in my vehicle- I've owned a car, a truck, and a van! Yes, I still have copies of the 2 CD sets and the cassette tape. Oh, and I had just about the entire music opera memorized.

Yes, I could sing the part of the Phantom, all of it! I sang Raoul, too, but I don't have that part memorized anymore. My version features Michael Crawford, Sarah Brightman, and Steve Barton; my CD jacket shows a 1987 The Really Useful Group P.L.C. version. Andrew Lloyd Weber was, and still is, one of my favorite composers. Besides "Phantom," there was, and they still are on my playlists, *Jesus Christ Super Star*, *Cats*, and *Joseph, and the Amazing Technicolor Dreamcoat*, which I often listened to. I grew up with, well, I listened to all of them, each as they came out. I remember an older version of "Phantom" that my cousins and I would watch as kids, and we would quote it. Gee, is black and white familiar?

I remember listening to various musicals, of one form or another, when I needed to get different tasks done, mostly housework and homework. Ultimately, I would sing one of the parts or another and would have accomplished a lot by the finale.

I remember the *Time Warp* from the Rocky Horror Picture Show would often get me going, and it gave me a smile, too. The emphasized division of the beat provides a driving force that can easily be transferred to an energized subdivision. It had a bit more of a relaxed "one" and "three" that still had its own groove style. The only way for me to explain it is to have you listen to it. I'll bet you'll do the dance at least once! If you are unfamiliar with the dance or the song, watch it on YouTube! It's astounding!

Picture 3:
Zeta Tau doing hotdogs at CU (circa 2011).

Ok, I talked about two musicals/musical theatre, a genre of music that addressed motivation, or lack thereof, an effect of PTSD. I enjoyed musicals regularly; however, there were times that I would listen to a specific song from a show or just let a show run. At times, particular songs would help me deal with stress or anxiety. At other times, I'd seek out an entire show. I remember that around the late 1990s, *Joseph and the Technicolor Dreamcoat* often lifted my spirits and made me feel better when I was feeling depressed or not feeling particularly motivated. It was as if experiencing betrayal and hardship, then reunification and forgiveness vicariously assisted me in dealing with those issues.

Musical theatre wasn't the only genre I listened to; *Man of La Mancha* was my first musical, and *Carmen* was my first opera. I'll now toss a few songs/compositions that would also help me.

One work, lasting around 15 minutes, is the *1812 Overture* by Pyotr Ilyich Tchaikovsky. It opened with strings, soft and smooth. This theme would later be stated in a much broader and more exciting presentation, complete with church and orchestra bells, but that's later in the piece. For now, I'm listening to soft and smooth strings. This opening section has a clearly heard subdivision providing motion and a feeling of calm breathing. This grows in intensity, just a little, and provides a sense of direction- forward. Around 2:00 or so, the underlying subdivision accelerates until brass enters, sounding triumphant, stating, "I am here." This offers a sense of awareness and watchfulness. As the subdivision changes from duple to triple, my breathing continues as before, in for a few bars and then out for a few; however, the intensity of the melodic activity, the increase in instrumentation, and the emphasis that the brass provides enable me to feel a sense of new energy coming upon me. The strings take over with a link that leads to a familiar theme that is heard between the strings and the Horns. This is around 4:00 into the piece. As a Horn player, this also gives me that added boost from performing both the band and orchestra versions. Ah, memories, but I digress.

As I was saying, the theme in The Horns with the Strings gave me a feeling of some new energy and awareness. Then, the pause, the regrouping of my mind. The strings built upon the silence by stating a very rhythmic theme with many accented "and-one," eight notes that cross from the subdivision of a beat to the articulation of the next beat. This section also featured an active subdivision as an ostinato or accented counter melody. This provided me with some energy and a bit of motivation. Numerous ascending and descending scale patterns accompany the statement of the French National Anthem, and the theme is presented in various brass instruments. This is an active and semi-intense section. I say semi-intense because the finale is so much more so. But I digress again.

This section finally allows the trumpet to state the French National Anthem theme, followed by what is sometimes considered to represent the conflict between France and Russia. There are a lot of three rhythmic eighth-note notes followed by an eighth-note rest motif. This motif is sometimes presented with the rest on a beat and, at times, not, depending on the instrumentation and counterpoint. This pattern gave my mind a feeling of sorting out what was going on and a feeling of alertness. I find myself slowly feeling energized. However, this is built up only so much, but only a little. The strings take over with a flowing melody, with the accompaniment shaping my breathing, in and out by 2 bars and out by 2 bars. Long, deep breathing. This begins around 6:45 into the piece. The strings and woodwinds alternate motifs until they lead into a dance-like section, around 8:00, that faded until around 9:00 when the brass and strings restated some of the previous "conflict" material; this time, the percussion had a louder and more accenting role. By now, I'm feeling alert and motivated. I love the Horns around 10:00!

Around 10:30, there is a restatement of the flowing melody that leads to a return to and the fading of the other dancelike melody, even restating the earlier mentioned moment of silence. Then. At 11:30, the finale begins! At 12:00, I have goosebumps, thanks to the canons! Just before 12:50, it all comes to a head! The church bells! The Brass! The glory and magnificence of Tchaikovsky's composing! I have won many "barracks stereo wars" with this piece! Yes, I shook the SGM's office, two decks below and a few hundred feet away.

Chapter 3

My Graduate Years at CU

My "grad" years started with me taking a few introductory grad courses to fill out my last semester as an undergrad. There was a crossover semester that included both undergraduate and graduate school courses. Music, for me, took on additional meaning; memories and connections with family (wife and daughters) were established. Songs that once were happy and motivating for me later turned into melancholy songs that encouraged memories to fall down my cheeks. The passage of time and life circumstances can change the role of a song or music in your life; at times, it has mine. Music from this time and earlier times will change roles later. But, for now, we'll stay in this time frame.

One of my oldies but goodies is from my early military days in 1982. In the early 1990s, Yazoo's album Upstairs at Eric's faded from my playlist; however, it came back around 2000 and made a noticeable appearance in 2009. I would listen to and relate to one song in particular: *In My Room*. I feel obligated to print the words as they are presented in the CD literature.

In My Room
By Yazoo, V. Clarke

I stand alone and watch the clock
I only wait for it to stop
And in the room locked up inside me
The cut-out magazines remind me
I sit and wait alone in my room.
And in my room against the wall
There is a picture very small
A photograph I took some years ago
It shows a picture of a room I know
I sit and wait alone in my room

The walls are white and in the night
The room is lit by electric light

I stand alone and watch the clock
I only wait for it to stop
The doors are shut and all the windows lock
The only sound is from the clock
I sit and wait alone in my room.

The walls are white and in the night
The room is lit by electric light

This song is accompanied by "The Lord's Prayer," recited in the back-ground. It's ironic since many of the times I would listen to this song, it often involved me praying. This song would come to my mind during the times when I thought about dying, how you die, and the physical release of everything within. It also helped me through rough times when I did not know my purpose or why I was still around. The lyrics accurately described me and my life, especially around 2009 when I questioned myself. I had lost a very dear friend and was feeling lost and alone. I'm unsure how I would have made it if it weren't for my fraternity.

This song brings me from depression and contemplation to contemplation and self-reflection. The words "deliver us from evil" remind me that help is available, and I need to be receptive to His guidance and receive His protection. These words would make me remember that killing is an act of evil. It is wrong to kill oneself. I would also think about those I have lost. Not that I wanted to join them, but what would they want me to do? So far, every time, I conclude that those I have lost would like me to keep carrying on, playing my music, and being there for my Brothers and Sisters, Kappa Kappa Psi and Tau Beta Sigma, and veterans alike.

I have often thought the room described could be an inpatient room in a mental hospital setting. I realize this is most likely not the case; there is no mention of padding, and there is a picture. For me, the lyrics describe a veteran's room, a veteran who lives alone. The room described can belong to one of a thousand veterans. It could also describe my inner space and what things are like from my perspective. Could the "picture very small" refer to memories or experiences? I found the words to be relatable. *In My Room* has been with me for many years and has grounded me on many occasions.

The rhythmic ostinato, a triple subdivision, and the subsequent use of silence provided an underlying pattern to establish a relaxed breathing rate. The addition of the snare drum offers a sense of motion and movement. The lack of the rhythmic ostinato for the last six iterations of "but deliver us from evil" emphasizes the reflective nature of this song. The song ends with a request. In effect, it ends with a request for protection and guidance.

Picture 4:
Pep-Rally at CU, 2012.

When I needed motivation, I would listen to and often conduct Gustav Holst's *The Planets: Mars, the Bringer of War*. I enjoyed listening to the entire suite; different movements elicited different responses from and within me. However, one of my favorite movements is *Mars, the Bringer of War*. I may be biased because I am a Horn player. Naw, that can't be it.

What drives *Mars* is the rhythmic ostinato: triplet eight notes, two-quarter notes, a divided beat (simple-duple), and two-quarter notes. Each measure has five beats, with the quarter note receiving the beat. This starts in the percussion before some brass comes in with long tones outlining a long tone that changes on the second measure on the fourth beat held out for the rest of the measure. There are an eventual three plus two groups of beats that sway: 1-2-3, 4-5.

This ostinato continues building by adding instruments. There is a moment when the counterpoint is so intense that the additional textures and intensity increase, culminating in a swirl ascending that falls and lands on a closed position root and dominant, in the lower octaves of the strings and brass; and this is only 3:00 into the movement. This pedal tone faded as the snare drum picked up the rhythmic triplet and beat 4-5 as the low strings and woodwinds slowly built up in motion as soft trumpets called repeated eight-note triplets intermittently in the background.

Around 4:30, the ostinato is presented in the brass and strings before the low brass, woodwinds, and low strings enter at a very full fortissimo. This full orchestration presentation of the ostinato, the theme, and the counter theme is driven by a relentless snare drum that doesn't skip a beat. It drives on! Around 6:15, the piece climaxes with a very open-scored and thickly textured chord sequence that reduces in texture and intensity after each motif is presented. The movement closes with upper woodwinds and strings actively "scurrying" with the chords outlined as inverted arpeggios in a pattern that climbed up the scale, leading to the brass and wood-winds presenting a series of open-position chords. The moment of silence before the last chord, the root and dominant orchestrated in the lower octaves, emphasizes the finality of the last chord.

I listen to *Mars* for motivation and to help make tedious tasks tolerable. I can feel the drive of the compound meter, the breathing patterns of the three and two groupings, and the texture as it thickens during the more active moments, especially with the counterpoint. It also helps that I have performed this, band and orchestra versions, and conducted it many times. There is something about asking for and getting more out of an ensemble: fuller and more intense fortissimos and soft, smooth pianissimos. Listening to *Mars* wasn't the only way I was motivated by it.

Chapter 4

Music Between CU and OU

I had a wide selection on my playlists around 2003-2008. I spent much time listening to music from Europe and Celtic culture. Nature sounds were also frequently played. My different moods determined what I listened to. For example, if I were depressed, I would not listen to a song about war. I would listen to something much happier; the lyrics had a lot to determine this. I always liked Bagpipes.

And now for something completely different. Depeche Mode was often comforting to me. Their album Some Great Reward had two songs I frequently sought: *Somebody* and *Blasphemous Rumors*. Their songs *"People Are People"* and *"Master and Servant"* are others of my choice. Yes, this music is old music. It also speaks to emotions and states of mind; Emo music, only at this time, in 1984, was New Age/New Wave. I often found myself returning to the music I listened to when I was younger for comfort, for motivation, or to deal with my memories and demons.

Depeche Mode's song *Somebody* helped me deal with my feelings of depression when I felt like I was alone or if I was looking to feel as if I mattered to someone. The lyrics reminded me of what I was searching for—what many veterans search for after separating from the military. I must present the lyrics as they appear on the album's inner jacket; yes, I said album.

Somebody,
words, and music by M. L. Gore

I want somebody to share
Share the rest of my life
Share my innermost thoughts
Know my intimate details
Someone who'll stand by my side
And give me support
And in return
She'll get my support
She will listen to me
When I want to speak
About the world we live in
And life in general
Though my views may be wrong
They may even be perverted
She will hear me out
And won't easily be converted
To my way of thinking

In fact she'll often disagree
But at the end of it all
She will understand me

I want somebody who cares
For me passionately
With every thought and with every breath
Someone who'll help me see things
In a different light
All the things I detest
I will almost like
I don't want to be tied
To anyone's strings
I'm carefully trying to steer clear
Of those things
But when I'm asleep
I want somebody
Who will put their arms around me
And kiss me tenderly
Through things like this
Make me sick
In a case like this
I'll get away with it

The first verse is a statement of standards and expectations. Clearly stated, "understand me." Disagreement is acceptable, even expected; we are individuals, not copies. Interestingly, lyrics describe one who does not always agree, one who listens, supports, and understands. The second verse describes the more intimate side of a relationship. It describes one who cares passionately and intimately, who helps to see things in a "different light," and who will accept and show tenderness.

A veteran who is not used to this or has not felt this way can "almost like" this experience. The last few lines, "though things like this make me sick, in a case like this, I'll get away with it," describe the wall built around oneself being chipped away, at least in one spot. The song described what I could not clearly articulate. I could feel what I was looking for but could not describe it to myself or others. I knew that I wanted to let someone in, but only if they met specific criteria. I was able to acknowledge my thoughts and feelings, CBT in action. I could experience the moment and then move on with thoughts of hope.

Picture 5:
Peter Burke, 24 Aug 2009.

Other music from this time in my life included more music from my past. I would listen to the Beatles, *Here Comes the Sun*, for calm and comfort. I find the lyrics to be hopeful. I also like it when the division of the beat is grouped as a triplet-triplet-triplet-duple-duple pattern. The words "sun, sun, sun (each held over rhythmic triplets), here-we (duple) co-me (duple)."

Here are the lyrics:

Here Comes the Sun
By the Beatles, George Harrison

Here comes the sun, doo-doo-doo-doo
Here comes the sun, and I say
It's all right

Little darlin', it's been a long, cold, lonely winter
Little darlin', it feels like years since it's been here
Here comes the sun, doo-doo-doo-doo
Here comes the sun, and I say
It's all right

Little darlin', the smile's returning to their faces
Little darlin', it seems like years since it's been here
Here comes the sun
Here comes the sun, and I say
It's all right

Sun, sun, sun, here it comes
Sun, sun, sun, here it comes
Sun, sun, sun, here it comes
Sun, sun, sun, here it comes
Sun, sun, sun, here it comes

Little darlin', I feel that ice is slowly melting
Little darlin', it seems like years since it's been clear
Here comes the sun, doo-doo-doo-doo
Here comes the sun, and I say
It's all right

Here comes the sun, doo-doo-doo-doo
Here comes the sun
It's all right
It's all right

I also have memories associated with this song. I remember listening to this with my brother when we lived in Groton, CT, in Navy housing. I won't go into that particular childhood memory; however, it was playing when I wasn't feeling the greatest, and it helped. It may have been that this song was also associated with my brother during this time. I was in elementary school listening to the Beatles, the Doors, Simon and Garfunkel, Zappa, Led Zeppelin, the Beach Boys, and the Rolling Stones. My brother's music, mostly. He is, after all, 10 years older than me.

Chapter 5

Back to Grad School:
Music at the University of Oklahoma

I want to switch gears and talk about some music from OU, such as the chant and the fight song. Both hold a special place in my heart. I remember many times I would join when one group or another would take up our chant in the main foyer of Catlett Hall. The acoustics are fantastic! It would usually start with a small group, but soon, it filled up with students, faculty, and staff all joining in!

The chant was written in 1936 by Jessie Lone Clarkson. I remember that it is often sung before home football games and at official university functions. Here are the words:

O-K-L-A-H-O-M-A
Our chant rolls on and on!
Thousands strong
Join heart and song
In Alma Mater's praise
Of campus beautiful by day and night

Of colors proudly gleaming Red and White
'Neath a western sky
OU's chant will never die
Live on University!

I remember feeling at home when I was at OU. I felt as if I belonged. I recall these feelings every time I hear and sing our chant. When I hear it, I join in.

The fight song, *Boomer Sooner*, was written in 1905 by Arthur M. Alden. It can often be seen or heard at football games, more so in person than broadcast. Here are the words:

Boomer Sooner, Boomer Sooner
Boomer Sooner, Boomer Sooner
Boomer Sooner, Boomer Sooner
Boomer Sooner, OK U!

Oklahoma, Oklahoma
Oklahoma, Oklahoma
Oklahoma, Oklahoma
Oklahoma, OK U!

I'm a Sooner born and Sooner bred
And when I die, I'll be Sooner dead
Rah, Oklahoma, rah, Oklahoma!
Rah, Oklahoma, OK U!

Picture 6:
Guest Pass-28 November 2009.

I will talk about another genre that gets me going: marches. Stay with me; eventually, it'll make sense as to why here, eventually.

Talking about the music from OU leads me to think about the Pride of Oklahoma, which leads me back in time to the Pride of Ft. Sill. A university marching band led me to an Army band. Army bands perform marches. Many marches. So, so many marches. So, here I am talking about marches. Oh, don't get me wrong. Marches were performed at OU, but nothing like the US Army Bands!

Marches help me stay motivated or keep a steady pace when performing a task or function. Marches are an excellent way to pass the time when you must walk or run a long distance. I also listen to marches when I have things like housework to do. Listening to marches can take the monotony out of tasks. The form and structure of marches are very similar. They start in the tonic key for the first and second strains. The trio is usually in the dominant key. Depending on the march, the trio can have one or two strains, followed by a break-up strain or a "dogfight" before the last strain is presented.

Marches usually have two beats per measure, with a duple or triple division of each beat. The division of the beat, usually in the Horns, follows a pattern using a tuba or sousaphone for the downbeat, and the Horns, on the duple division, play an eighth note in the second half of the beat. The Horns play on the first, third, fourth, and sixth eight notes for a triple division.

Our national march is John Philip Sousa's *The Stars and Stripes Forever*. The piccolo solo in the Trio is familiar and often scored for other instruments as the soloist. I recommend looking up the solo as being played on a Tuba. I've played it on the Horn and felt like I ran a marathon. One must have dexterity and breath control to accomplish the solo.

Some motivating elements of marches are the Sousa-phone and bass drum (the bass line), the accompanying divisions, and the form that the Trio has. Usually, after the breakup strain or dogfight, the last strain is presented with a thick texture and intense volume, encompassing the full range of the staff.

One of my favorite marches to keep a steady pace/stay motivated is *British Eighth* by Zo Elliott. I usually sing it/hum it in my head around 106-110 beats per minute: definitely slower than 112 beats per minute. It has a form, as described earlier. I especially enjoy the theme in the trio. I usually played the melody despite the conductor. In fact, almost every Horn player in the Army bands I have been in took it upon ourselves to "improvise" our part. Some of us even had it coordinated as a section. This was especially true for *March Grandioso* by Roland F. Seitz, but I'm digressing.

Back to *British Eighth*. The second strain contrasts with the first strain's smoother, more regal statement. This strain is much more articulated, especially in the accompaniment; this features the low brass with the melody in this strain. The smoother presentation is added to the articulated accompaniment as the march leads into the trio. The Trio is fun to "improvise." This melody is smooth and flowing, with a soft bugle call in the background. Now comes the breakup strain; I call this one a dogfight due to its heavy articulation and instrumental scoring. This leads to the theme in the trio, the last strain. The theme returns with a thicker texture and fuller sound at a slightly slower, slightly more grandiose tempo, a statelier tempo, and presentation. The big difference is that I don't play stingers! I don't conduct them! Usually.

Ok, I mentioned it, so I may as well discuss it, *March Grandioso*, by Roland F. Seitz. This is one march that I and others improvised on. We would play the part melody, toss some countermelody, and part accompaniment. We made our parts very enjoyable to play. Yes, we did our triple division pattern now and again. I learned this when I was with the 7th at Ft. Ord. We were bored and started improvising for fun. Not too much, at first. Occasionally, we'd get a look from the conductor, but that didn't deter us. We would tone it back and play more of our divided beat patterns if needed. We kept it within the melodic or countermelody, and, most importantly, we kept it musical. Eventually, while I was with the 25th, we were "improvising" as a section. This carried over to my time in the 10th, but I didn't worry about the looks this time. My tongue was sharp and on the forward edge. Give me those triple-division arpeggiated passages! When I went to the 77th, I ran into Horn players who knew the improvisations. They didn't have to "learn" it. Oh, by the way, I've performed this at tempos ranging from 110 to 120 and maybe a tad more. If you have not heard of *March Grandioso*, I suggest you watch it on YouTube.

One song that I'd like to talk about is Simon and Garfunkel's *Sound of Silence*. I had a life event that brought the darkness back into my world. Here are the lyrics:

The Sound of Silence
By Simon and Garfunkel, Paul Simon

Hello darkness, my old friend
I've come to talk with you again
Because a vision softly creeping
Left its seeds while I was sleeping
And the vision that was planted in my brain
Still remains
Within the sound of silence

In restless dreams, I walked alone
Narrow streets of cobblestone
'Neath the halo of a street lamp
I turned my collar to the cold and damp
When my eyes were stabbed by the flash of a neon light
That split the night
And touched the sound of silence

And in the naked light, I saw
Ten thousand people, maybe more
People talking without speaking
People hearing without listening
People writing songs that voices never shared
No one dared
Disturb the sound of silence

"Fools," said I, "You do not know
Silence like a cancer grows
Hear my words that I might teach you
Take my arms that I might reach you"
But my words like silent raindrops fell
And echoed in the wells of silence

And the people bowed and prayed
To the neon god they made
And the sign flashed out its warning
In the words that it was forming
And the sign said, "The words of the prophets are
written on the subway walls
In tenement halls"
And whispered in the sounds of silence

I listen to this song when I am down or depressed. I acknowledge my thoughts and feelings, and then I can deal with my demons. The lyrics describe many of my thoughts when I think about things: loss, pain, and wondering, "Why?" Silence. Words of guidance and comfort were provided, yet not. Echoes. And more silence. I am usually calm and reflective by the end.

Chapter 6

Music During My Doctorate Travels

By now, it's around 2012-2015. Ok, not really. Music during my doctoral journey and the subsequent time since is, and has been, more music from my past. I have always listened to nature sounds or other meditation-type music. I prefer to go hiking. Ok, I like to go walking in the woods. I want to find a quiet spot to sit and listen. Nature is very melodic if you listen. Camping at night is often a symphony of nature. Since I don't have the camping opportunities I used to, my backyard or my back porch is often a front-row seat in the concert hall.

My music playlist is very eclectic. My selections vary depending on my location. For example, I may listen to *Fanfare for the Common Man* by Aaron Copeland when I'm alone, but if I'm in a group, I may listen to nature sounds or something more appropriate for a social setting. Sorry, but not all social settings would suit Frank Zappa, especially for the song I am currently thinking about.

At times, I would listen to specific music for specific recall or a particular feeling I want to experience. Sometimes, I would find myself singing in German; most often, it would be Peter Schilling or Schumann. Ok, maybe Beethoven, but I digress. Peter Schilling's album *Error in the System* has several selections I often include on my playlist, such as *Only Dreams*, *The Noah Plan*, and *Major Tom (Coming Home)*. His version of *Stille Nacht, Heilige Nacht (Silent Night, Holy Night)*, has new words set to the traditional tune.

Stille Nacht, Heilige Nacht (Silent Night, Holy Night)
By Peter Schilling

Stille Nacht, heilige Nacht
Alles um uns rum ist satt
Nur auf der anderen Seite der Welt
Ist der Becher voll Reis
Der das Leben erhält

Dort kommt durch Hunger die Not
Durch unsere Waffen der Tod

Stille Nacht, heilige Nacht
Die Schwachen das schwach sein bewusster macht
Die Kinder durch Schenken die Liebe ersetzt
Die Mütter vor betrunkenen Vätern beschützt

Wo man zu Tränen gerührt
Einmal im Jahr dem Pfarrer zuhört

Stille Nacht, heilige Nacht
Selbst heute werden wir bewacht
Weil keiner mehr richtig dem anderen vertraut
Man statt Vertrauen nur Grenzen aufbaut

Und man die Bombe kaum hört
Die uns langsam von innen zerstört

Stille Nacht, heilige Nacht
Irgendwo wird grad einer umgebracht
Im Namen des Friedens, des Glaubens, der Macht
Wird grad eine Waffe in Stellung gebracht
Schließet Augen und Ohren fest zu
Beschert euch weiter in seliger

Here is an English translation. The words may seem "dark" to some; however, I profoundly reflect on the translated lyrics. The instrumentation features a string bass predominantly as the accompaniment, with a high hat on the drum set, keeping time for the triple division of the beat. I'll leave the English translation here.

Silent Night, Holy Night
Everything around us is full
Only on the other side of the world

Is the cup full of rice
that sustains life
There comes hardship
through hunger Death through our weapons

Silent Night, Holy Night
The weak make them more aware of being weak
The children replaced by giving love
The mothers protected
from drunken fathers
Where you are moved to tears
Once a year you listen to the priest

Silent Night, Holy Night
Even today we are guarded
Because no one really trusts
the other anymore Instead of trust, you only build
borders
And you can hardly hear
the bomb slowly destroying
us from the inside

Silent Night, Holy Night
Somewhere someone is being killed
In the name of peace, faith, power
A weapon is just being brought
into position. Close your eyes and ears tightly
Give yourselves further in blissful rest

Picture 7:
Peter Burke, around 2016.

At this point, I intended to write about Lynyrd Skynyrd's *Free Bird*. This song from my childhood was often played at our school dances. Just picture a bunch of junior high school kids dancing to this in the gym; it's slow, excellent music to get to know someone, and then it ramps up like mad! The guitar solo is fantastic! The melody ramps up and accelerates a little at around 5:00 into the piece. From there on, it's all guitar solo! Yes, a little more than 4:00 of pure, unadulterated rock! I'm usually very motivated by the end. Enough said. After all, this is classic rock at its best.

So, instead of talking about *Free Bird*, I'd like to talk about other alternative types of "music" I listen to when I want to "get myself right." I specifically want to mention the many international selections on my playlist. My heritage is Italian. My last name is Burke, an Irish name. Yes, you guessed it, I enjoy Celtic music. I listen to Enya, the Celtic Woman, Drop Kick Murphys, and the Coors, to name a few. As I have said, there are times when my setting or location, or my goal for listening, may determine what selection I listen to at that time.

I also enjoy listening to Russian Church music, especially the basses. I particularly enjoy feeling the notes throughout my body and hearing that low pedal rumble. I also enjoy Alfred Reed's *Russian Christmas Music*. No, it is not Russian, but it just came to mind. It is a great piece to perform, especially for Horn players! I recommend it on YouTube.

The other international works on my playlist are from Germany, Korea, Australia, Israel, and Africa, to name a few. The music on your playlist must be meaningful to you, or it will not do you any good.

Chapter 7

My Music-Based Support System in My Academic Journey: Kappa Kappa Psi- Zeta Tau; Delta; Zeta Tau

If you have read my previous book, *A Student-Veteran's Experience with Higher Education: An Academic Journey*, some of this may be a review, just some. See if you can find the added material, lol.

Ok, so here is one of my most prominent music-based support groups. Kappa Kappa Psi (KKY) Fraternity was founded on the campus of Oklahoma State University in 1919 to serve the College and University band programs. I joined the Zeta Tau (ZT) Chapter of KKY on December 22, 1997, at Cameron University in Lawton, Oklahoma. Our mission was to support the CU Instrumental program.

Picture 8:
KKY SW District Convention, 6-8 Apr 2001.

I had a fantastic experience with my ZT Brothers! I instantly became the oldest and developed relationships that are still with me 25 years later. We supported each other as a family and established music and social relationships that lasted for years.

I was an active member of ZT from 1997-2001, when I received my diploma. I stayed active in ZT as a graduate student until the summer of 2003 and became an Alumni Member. The ZT Chapter folded during the 2003-04 academic year before I returned to CU to work in the FAL&ML. It was later re-formed as a Colony in 2009 and became a Chapter on October 8, 2011; I was the Colony's Vice-President in 2010 and the Chapter's first President in 2011, the Alpha class of this newly established Chapter.

During my time at OU, I was an Alumni Member of the Delta Chapter (alumni of ZT, Epsilon series—I wish I could remember the specific class designation); I later became an Active Member for the 2009-2010 academic year. I was again instantly the oldest member of the chapter. I was welcomed with open arms and accepted as a Brother, even though I could be some of the members' fathers.

Picture 9:
Me at "The Caboose" - 2010

We supported the instrumental program much as the ZT chapter did, with one big difference: unlike Cameron University, OU has a football team! Much logistics had to be accomplished before the Pride even set foot on the field; the Delta chapter and our Sisters of Tau Beta Sigma (TBS), the band sorority, filled those positions and areas of responsibilities.

While a member of Delta, I attended as many events as I possibly could; I drove over an hour one way to school from my house in Elgin. My Brothers understood when I had to leave early or if I could not attend an event. I was working and living a long way away. I did a "day trip" each day of the SW District Convention held at OU for the 2009-2010 year; I would have liked to stay over-night in Norman, but I could not find anyone to take care of my animals, so I went home every night. The combined Delta Chapters of Kappa Kappa Psi and Tau Beta Sigma hosted the convention and did an excellent job!

Picture 10:
Kappa Kappa Psi- Zeta Tau, Alpha class, 2010/2011.

In the summer of 2010, I received a call from a student I knew while working at CU to find out if I wanted to be a part of resurrecting the ZT Chapter at CU. I returned to CU to take R/TV classes to improve my broadcasting and editing skills. I served as the ZT Colony Vice-

President for the 2010-2011 year and then its first Chapter President in the 2011-2012 academic year.

My affiliation with Kappa Kappa Psi has inspired me and sometimes carried me through some rough memories. Whether performing music, conducting music, listening to music, or talking about music, I could feel the support provided.

One of the best parts of my academic journey was my affiliation with Kappa Kappa Psi. It gave me a sense of belonging to a family and provided me with a support system that I never had before. I was quickly accepted into the Brotherhood, and my age and experience contributed to the activities and musical growth experienced at both of my chapters. I could not have asked for a better music-based support system than with my Brothers and Sisters.

Picture 11:
My Life Membership Pin for Kappa Kappa Psi.

The music of KKY provided me with a feeling of belonging and comfort, especially our Hymn. I often hummed it or softly sang it when I felt alone or needed to remember that I was cared about; no matter where I was, I would always have my brothers, Zeta Tau or Delta. My copies of my sheet music are a bit worn, which I could find (KKY and my music from CU and OU), so I downloaded clean versions of the Fraternity Song and the Fraternity Hymn.

The Fraternity Song was approved by the National Chapter in 1975 and then arranged by Todd Malicoate in 1987; this is the version I am familiar with. This version started with a soothing "ooh" in G-flat, modulating to A-flat. It was later arranged by the Ritual and Regalia Committee in 2015. The latest version does not have the choral style "oohs." This version starts with the tune in the key of A, which was arranged by Kevin Day in 2019.

The Fraternity Hymn was adopted by the National Chapter in 1995 before I retired, but I digress. It was based on the hymn "*Someday*" with words by, and arranged by, Scott Jeffrey Heckstall, Jr., Eta Gamma chapter, 1977. To this day, I still have "memories" roll down my face whenever I hear our hymn. YouTube videos are my most common source since I have trouble finding sound files/recordings from back in the day. I can sing it, hear the other parts in my head, and be brought back in time. There have been times in my life when this hymn provided comfort when I felt alone or when I wondered who, if anyone, cared about me. Remembering that I am not alone and that I am part of a more prominent Brotherhood helped me make it through the rough times (personal life, PTSD, depression).

Chapter 8

Duality

As I mentioned, music can have dual roles, depending on where you are in your time-space continuum. I found myself watching an episode of NCIS. I forgot the name, but it was about a sniper, Musicorp, and PTSD; Tim was worried Delilah had his phone- about the engagement ring, and the episode had the song *Halleluia* on at the end. I'll find out the version of the song and the episode name later; I don't want to digress too far (yes, I'm typing just after the episode aired); if I discussed this earlier, fantastic; if not, sweet. I'm writing this chapter before I may discuss *Halleluia* earlier in my life. At least, I believe I am.

I would listen to *Halleluia* by Jeff Buckley when I felt wound up, anxious, or needed- in some way, shape, form, or fashion- to calm down. It had often provided me with a sense of focus; the chord progression in the beginning, Dominant seventh – Tonic progression (I think. I'm trying to remember the voicing, bass note, inversion), had that slight tendency to lead from one chord to the other; it lent itself to a subtle "sway" each "sway" facilitated an even breathing which led to a calming effect, at least, for me.

The lyrics had their own calming effect. It had something to do with me being a composer and performer. That "minor fall and the major lift" brings me back to my composer days, visualizing a score. I remember the steady macro-beat; the micro was not very often prominent; when it was, it was often a division leading to the next chord to act as a link; otherwise, it was a soft arpeggio. This song has many versions and covers from the movie *Shrek*, television (an episode of NCIS comes to mind), YouTube, and the concert venue. So far, I have not found one that did not move me.

Now, all it takes is for me to hear the intro, and I can feel the memories start to build. It does not take long for them to escape and roll down my cheek(s). I'm not sure why or what memory escapes; they are often different, yet many repeat. I remember old friends that are no longer here; damn, I miss them. I think about times when this song was attached to good memories from my past, memories of events that can never happen again, and memories of people I miss.

What was once calming, focusing, and relaxing was now, very often, bringing sad-ness and feelings of melancholy or depression. I have found that simple arrangements, small ensembles, are incredibly effective at drawing out an emotional response.

Picture 12:
My view-19 Sep 2009.

OK, it's later. *God Bless the USA*, by Lee Greenwood, started to be a song of patriotism and motivation. I related to the lyrics; however, the time of my life determines how things go within me. Do I cry in sadness due to remembrance, or do I cry due to a sense of loss? Are the memories that roll down my cheek fond memories of people, places, and times? Or are they drifting back in time of grief? Memories are triggered by sight, smell, and sound. I can usually tell where my mindset is heading when I hear the introduction. I have been unable to sing it all through without choking up for many years. I'll leave it at that.

Here are the lyrics. You will see why this song has a duality in interpretation and emotional meaning for me.

God Bless the USA
By Lee Greenwood

If tomorrow all the things were gone
I worked for all my life
And I had to start again
With just my children and my wife
I'd thank my lucky stars
To be livin' here today
'Cause the flag still stands for freedom
And they can't take that away
And I'm proud to be an American
Where at least I know I'm free
And I won't forget the men who died
Who gave that right to me
And I'd gladly stand up
Next to you and defend her still today
'Cause there ain't no doubt I love this land
God bless the USA

From the lakes of Minnesota
To the hills of Tennessee
Across the plains of Texas
From sea to shining sea
From Detroit down to Houston

And New York to L.A.
Well, there's pride in every American heart
And it's time we stand and say

That I'm proud to be an American
Where at least I know I'm free
And I won't forget the men who died
Who gave that right to me
And I'd gladly stand up
Next to you and defend her still today
'Cause there ain't no doubt I love this land (love this land)
God bless the USA

And I'm proud to be an American
Where at least I know I'm free
And I won't forget the men who died
Who gave that right to me
And I'd gladly stand up
Next to you and defend her still today
'Cause there ain't no doubt I love this land (love this land)
God bless the USA

As a veteran, this song reminds me of my brothers and sisters from the military. It reminds me of the pride my family has in being citizens of this country. This song reminds me of my dad's pride in being a part of the Submarine Service. I was incredibly proud of him. My dad loved us a great deal. But he loved our country a bit more. He would say not to take things for granted. To stand up for what is right. He loved our country and passed that love of country on to us.

Chapter 9

Issues and Concerns - A Support System: Why a Music-based Support System is Important

Mrs. Jennifer Parrish, MA, BCBA, LBA, has reviewed the information in chapters 9 and 10 of this manuscript for data accuracy, interpretation, and removal of researcher bias. Here is what I discovered during my research.

Some of this information has been used in my previous book about my academic journey, putting things in context for those who have not read *A Student-Veteran's Experience with Higher Education: An Academic Journey*. Oh, I added new material here, as well.

During my academic journey, especially in the 21st century, I observed that student-veterans have consistently increased. The US Census Bureau and the Department of Veterans Affairs (VA) validate my observation. The student-veteran is becoming a more significant percentage of the total student population in the United States, almost 4%. Many student-veterans left a part of themselves in a distant place, some in places civilians will never hear about. Still, student-veterans are transitioning to the civilian world to advance their career development or to start a new one. Student-veterans carry the physical, emotional, and psychological scars from their past life experiences with them every day, escaping and constantly alone. They often feel isolated and alone. It is essential to consider what was given and to give back.

I retired from the military in 1996, and by the time I enrolled in school in 1997, I had deteriorated dramatically; I retired at 128 pounds, and my best weight in the military was 132, maybe 135. I had lost what little body fat I had and some muscle mass. For me, transitioning back into the civilian world was not easy. I call it "the year of hell." I was one of the many veterans who had issues and did not cope very well with memories, life events, or mental health upon separation. My life events include divorce and subsequent substance use, which then contributed to the demise of a once confident veteran and turned me into a statistic on the path to failure with no future. I noticed this change due to a compliment about looking good and asking if I had gained weight. I weighed myself and found I was 98 pounds—thirty pounds or so less than when I retired. Stress, depression, substance usage, and hanging out with other veterans who were also on the same destructive path as I was were all wake-up factors for me. I had lost about 30 lbs. since my retirement. I hadn't realized my civilian life was consumed by stress, depression, and substance use, alongside other veterans in similar situations that assisted in the weight loss.

I was lucky to have "informal" or unofficial support groups during my academic journey, specifically, my Brothers of Kappa Kappa Psi and the Sisters of Tau Beta Sigma. I shared a musical bond, which enabled me to connect with students who were not veterans; however, they still listened to my jokes and accepted me for who and what I am.

I recall a few times, especially around Memorial Day, that I would remember all the military funerals I played for. I would often look like I was a thousand miles away, and a few times, I was caught with a tear rolling down my cheek. I remember one year when I had a Zeta Tau member come and sit with me. No words. Just sat. Eventually, he raised his cup (we both were drinking coffee) and offered a slight silent nod as a toast. We drank. We sat for a few more minutes. Then we stood, smiled, said goodbye, and went our separate ways. I was fortunate that I had an informal, fraternal support system- my fraternity. A more formal structured support system is music or music therapy.

This summary provides background information on the history and development of music therapy, PTSD, and music mood and emotion. Veterans can experience the effect of their PTSD outside of a clinical setting and often will turn to a comfortable method of addressing their self-care; one common method is to listen to music. Music can alter moods or provide mental or emotional comfort. Some therapy methodologies include employing a music therapy-based approach in addressing the effects of PTSD (Gooding & Langston, 2019; Landis-Shack et al., 2017).

In assembling literature for this study, the researcher discovered that existing literature that addresses music therapy and PTSD, or specifically the effects of PTSD, was not commonly available. Much of the literature found was about music therapy-based treatments or literature reviews on music therapy. It was common to find literature that stated the need for continued research relating to music therapy and PTSD; some literature recommended specificity in the study of music therapy about PTSD (Drozd, 2020; Peters et al., 2023).

Echezona (2023) reviewed music therapy's effectiveness in treating psychological conditions. The researcher provided a brief definition and history of music therapy and then discussed numerous psychological conditions: anxiety disorder, depression, PTSD, schizophrenia, bipolar disorder, and substance use disorder. The researcher concluded that music therapy can be effective as a treatment tool for psychological conditions and that more research is needed in this area.

Huang and Li (2022) reviewed the effects and applications of music therapy on psychological health. The researchers discussed music therapy as it related to emotions, both positive and negative, stress, anxiety, and pain. The following section covered different types of treatment, such as Behavioral, Humanistic, and Psychodynamic therapy. The last section addressed the application of music therapy as it pertains to ASD, Depression, and PTSD. The researchers concluded that it is likely that music therapy can stand out independently in the future. The researchers recommended that future research may focus on the psychological effects of different styles of music. The therapeutic effects of various genres have not received enough attention in the available research. Music Therapy has been adapted to successfully treat patients with psychological disorders, such as PTSD (Huang & Li, 2022).

Gooding and Langston (2019) reviewed music therapy with military populations; however, they did not mention the specific effects of PTSD. The researchers used a methodological framework in reviewing the literature that met their criteria, including reports, case studies, clinical program descriptions, and research studies. The historical reviews emphasized the historical connection between the development of music therapy and military personnel dating back to WWI, becoming officially recognized by the Music Therapy Association in the 1940s (Gooding & Langston, 2019).

Thomas and Chichaya (2023) reviewed the literature on the therapeutic use of music with military populations experiencing PTSD. The researchers stated that music can be a positive methodology for mental health settings; however, available literature on the use of music in occupational therapy is scarce. The authors concluded that combining occupational therapy with music therapy could maximize the effective-ness of music for people with mental health conditions. The authors list concerns and limitations to consider when applying the music component of the treatment, such as monitoring to prevent outbursts, aggressive behaviors, or relapses.

Findings from Thomas and Chichaya (2023) indicated that the therapeutic use of music allowed veterans to understand and regulate their emotions, reduce destructive behaviors, and reduce negative emotions. An understanding of emotions enables veterans to describe their feelings better, control their choices, and express the struggles that they have felt or are feeling. Songs facilitate the expression of struggles and hope for the future, facilitating improvement of their self/well-being. Music was also found to have a calming effect on mood, allowing distraction from stressors. One challenge was to enable veterans to express rage and not pose a risk of harm. Further research is needed to gain a deeper insight into the use of music therapy in the military population and how this can support PTSD (Thomas & Chichaya, 2023).

Drozd (2020) researched the therapeutic approach to military culture from a music therapist's perspective. This paper outlined the importance of military culture competency when practicing music therapy with veterans. Music therapy can help veterans learn and use beneficial coping skills to express their feelings and emotions better and has been shown to be a positive tool in addressing trauma and reestablishing identity (Drozd, 2020).

Bronson et al. (2018) studied music therapy treatment of active-duty personnel, an overview of intensive out-patient and longitudinal care programs. The researchers stated that it is essential for music therapists to provide effective treatment models in a military setting. Out-lining such models is critical to adding music therapy as a treatment tool for service members' complex injuries. Music perception research has identified the role of specific musical structures, such as tonality, timbre, and tempo, in music-evoked emotional responses (Bronson et al., 2018).

Landis-Shack et al. (2017) conducted a theoretical review of music therapy for PTSD in adults. The review described the practices of music therapy, including a historical view, as a treatment tool for addressing the symptoms of PTSD. Activities that promote music therapy's benefit as a treatment tool were discussed. It was concluded that music therapy may be a valuable tool in reducing symptoms and improving the functioning of individuals with PTSD. Music therapy may also help to alleviate the stigma of seeking treatment for PTSD (Landis-Shack et al., 2017).

Ophir and Jacoby (2020) conducted a qualitative investigation of musicking as a means of coping in adults with PTSD, investigating the performance of musical activity among those with PTSD. The meaning of musicking lies in the relationship established between the participants by the performance. The interviews identified two themes: musicking as an intra-subjective experience and musicking as a mediator of inter-subjective relationships. Three subordinate themes also emerged: musicking is a safe place, musicking is a dialectic experience, and musicking effectively bridges the past with the present to move toward the future. Musicking is a secure place for the wounded warrior. The authors recommended musicking as a therapeutic tool for people coping with the effects of PTSD (Ophir & Jacoby, 2020).

Hakvoort et al. (2020) studied music therapy to regulate arousal and attention in patients with substance use disorders and post-traumatic stress disorder. This study did not cover music selections addressing the effects of PTSD. The researchers acknowledged that the use of rhythm in music therapy could be clinically relevant in the treatment of individuals with PTSD. The literature reviewed did not indicate results for music therapy as a treatment for PTSD to date.

Baker et al. (2018) conducted a systemic review of the efficacy of creative arts therapies, such as music therapy, in the treatment of adults with PTSD. This review found that the quality of the trials is generally poor and that trials with more scientific rigor are needed in this area so that the effectiveness of treating the effects of PTSD can be more fully established. The researchers did note that at the end of the treatment period, there was a reduction in PTSD symptoms compared to the control group.

Bensimon (2020) discussed the perceptions of music therapists regarding their work with children living under continuous war threats and the reframing of trauma through songs. This study does discuss the benefits of the song in the study with children; however, it does not discuss music and the effects of PTSD. The topic of music therapy to treat children dealing with trauma has received little attention in music therapy research. Three themes emerged regarding the use of songs: 1) focuses on creating a playful and joyful space; 2) focuses on restoring a sense of control; and 3) fostering resilience, which relates to the ability of the song to address aspects of the traumatic experience and build a sense of strength. As a result, the traumatic experience was perceived as less threatening (Bensimon, 2020).

Peters et al. (2023) conducted a systemic review and meta-analysis of the impact of musicking on emotion regulation. Music serves functions that include emotion regulation, self-expression, and social bonding. Music is used to either enhance one's mood or to change one's mood. Participants in one reviewed study were proficient at using music for self-care daily.

Peters et al. (2023) defined emotion regulation as the process individuals employ to influence their emotions when they have them and how they choose to express their feelings. Music does impact the neural areas identified in processing emotions; however, the impact was not measured. Results in the literature supported the use of music to facilitate emotion regulation. More research into the effects of musicking on emotion regulation is needed.

Pant et al. (2022) conducted a review of the neurobio-logical framework for the therapeutic potential of music and sound interventions for post-traumatic stress symptoms in critical illness survivors. The authors summarized 19 studies employing neuroimaging measurements and a summary of the evidence from 12 studies on the effects of music interventions in patients with PTSD symptoms. The authors also provide an overview of PTSD-relevant brain areas, structural changes, and effects on behavior. Implementing music interventions in usual care has no adverse effects and can reduce ICU costs and facilitate effective management of PTSD with fewer sedative medications. Clinical evidence supports that relaxation music can help with coping and psychological transitioning after release from the ICU (Pant et al., 2022).

Capezuti et al. (2022) systematically reviewed auditory stimulation and sleep. The authors defined White noise, Pink noise, and "multi-audio interventions" that use either white or pink noise combined with music or silence. Music facilitates relaxation and distraction from stressful thoughts about one's situation. The authors provided tables summarizing the characteristics of their chosen 34 studies: 18 addressed White Noise, 11 addressed Pink Noise, and 6 addressed multi-audio studies.

White noise combines sounds of all different frequencies that are all at the same intensity level. White noise is used to decrease the audibility of background noise and treat tinnitus. Examples include video static, hiss from a radiator, or the sound of a fan. Pink noise contains all frequencies, but the intensity decreases as the frequency increases. Bass frequencies are louder, and high frequencies are turned down. Examples include nature sounds, such as ocean waves breaking on the shore or rustling leaves in the trees (Capezuti et al., 2022).

History and Development of Music Therapy

Music therapy has been documented as early as the ancient Greeks and Egyptians. Aristotle wrote that flute music could arouse strong emotions and purify the soul. Another early documented use of music therapy is in 1 Samuel 16, the story of David playing a harp to heal Saul. In the 19th century, the first use of music therapy in a large group setting for mentally ill patients was documented (Echezona, 2023).

The American Music Therapy Association defines music therapy as the clinical and evidence-based use of music to address emotional, cognitive, and social needs (Drozd, 2020; Echezona, 2023). Music therapy originates in military settings dating back to WWI and WWII; medical applications for music first appeared in collegiate training programs at Columbia University in 1919. More than 500 music therapists were trained between 1941 and 1944. By 1946, most available VA hospitals used music to treat the wounded; 44 VA hospitals had full-time music therapists on staff. This laid the groundwork in music therapy for standardization and regulation of music therapy as a profession (Bronson et al., 2018).

One approach to music therapy emphasizes social integration via music and the Guided Imagery in Music Technique. This involves listening to selected music to elicit imagery, symbols, and unconscious feelings (Landis-Shack et al., 2017).

Music therapy can be structured to meet the support needs utilizing a variety of instruments, mediums, and methods of expression. Music therapy is an acceptable method of treating individuals with PTSD. Music therapy may offer a more accessible and less stigmatizing therapeutic option for treating PTSD (Landis-Shack et al., 2017).

In music therapy, a therapeutic relationship must be formed with the client to improve mental health and personal goals. This relationship is needed to address the client's social, cognitive, and behavioral needs. Music therapy is a process in which therapists are trained to employ music as a treatment tool (Echezona, 2023).

The creation of the National Association for Music Therapists and the Certification Board of Music Therapists led to the standardization and accreditation of music therapists in the 1950s. Mental health providers must refer clients to music therapists if they want to include music therapy as a treatment method (Landis-Shack et al., 2017). Notable music programs that have partnerships with the Department of Defense (DoD) and the National Endowment for the Arts (NEA) include Resounding Joy's Semper Sound Military Music program, established in 2010, and the NEA Creative Forces Military Healing Arts Network, established in 2012 (Bronson et al., 2018).

PTSD

PTSD symptoms can be grouped into three categories: 1) invasiveness and re-experiencing the trauma, often as flashbacks, dreams, thoughts, and emotional distress; 2) avoidance of people, places, activities, and thoughts of the experience; and 3) hyper-arousal, often involving tension, sleep disorders, difficulty in concentration (often affecting job performance or academic perform-ance), and outbursts of anger. PTSD can often appear with other disorders, such as depression, anxiety, and social disorders (Ophir & Jacoby, 2020). The diagnosis of PTSD was not placed in the Diagnostics and Statistical Manual (DSM) until 1980 (Drozd, 2020). PTSD is an outcome of a process that encodes traumatic memories, cognitively and perceptually, and is disassoc-iated from other memories (Landis-Shack et al., 2017; Ophir & Jacoby, 2020).

PTSD is often complex to treat due to the trauma's effect on the brain (Ophir & Jacoby, 2020). Between January and June of 2000, the number of PTSD diagnoses included 39,264 non-deployed and 138,197 deployed personnel (De Los Santos et al., 2019; Osborne, 2016). Between 2000 and 2014, 149,000 new cases of PTSD were diagnosed within the Military Health System (Bronson et al., 2018). The Veterans Benefits Administration Annual Benefit Report, 2020, does not list statistics on the current number of non-service-connected diagnoses of PTSD (U.S. Department of Veterans Affairs, 2020b).

According to the VA 2020 Annual Benefits Report, 45,153 new beneficiaries received mental health benefits for PTSD, adding to the 1,186,818 total PTSD compensation recipients. The report also listed PTSD as a condition reported by 3.1% of new compensation recipients and 4.1% of all compensation recipients. The report's data only reflected service-connected compensations. No information was available in the report or supplemental files for non-service-related disability benefits (U.S. Department of Veterans Affairs, 2020a, 2020b, 2020c).

Music, Mood, and Emotions

The Romantic Era of music is known for music convey-
ing pictures and emotions. Beethoven's 6th Symphony,
the *Pastoral*, is a musical statement of a scene from life in
the country; Beethoven called it an expression of
feelings. The movements are often called *Merrymaking of
the Peasants*, *Storm*, and *Thankful Feelings after the Storm*
(Grout, 1980; Stolba, 1998). The numerous combina-
tions of the selection of music or instrumenta-tion that
can comprise the performing ensemble (including
vocal), the utilization of instruments/voices for effect or
imitation, and the scoring of the various instruments are
concepts that music composers keep in mind when
composing for a desired feeling or effect. For example,
the flute, oboe, and clarinet often imitate birds, such as
a nightingale, the quail, or the cuckoo. Texturing is
essential for establishing an effect or mood (Benjamin et
al., 1992; Grout, 1980; Kennan & Grantham, 1997;
Stolba, 1998).

The Doctrine of Affections was based on the philosophy
that music could move and affect the body. This theory
heavily influenced composers in the Baroque period and
how they composed music (Jarboe, 2018). Emotion is
evoked from the music, not the composer. Music can
affect the character and behavior of a person (Bensimon,
2020; Bronson et al., 2018; Jarboe, 2018; Landis-Shack
et al., 2017). This draws from the Doctrine of Ethos and

the characteristics found in the various music scales (Jarboe, 2018).

Different scales and modes have different characteristics, such as happy or sad. There are various types of scales, major and minor, often employed by composers to indicate happiness or sadness. Music frequently enhances or sets the mood of a scene, notably for films and movies. The Ionian mode is the major scale, with no alterations of the notes on the piano, all white keys from "C" to "C." Lydian and Mixolydian are the other major modes; white key "F" to "F" and "G" to "G," having a raised 4th scale degree and a lowered 7th scale degree from the Ionian, respectively (Benjamin et al., 1992; Ottman, 2004).

The Dorian, Aeolian, and Phrygian modes are the minor modes, Aeolian being the structure of natural minor, having a lowered 3rd, 6th, and 7th scale degree of the Ionian mode. Melodic minor and harmonic minor are variations of the natural minor. These alterations transform the happy tonality of the major scale into the sad tonality of a minor scale. The Locrian mode has a white key scale from "B" to "B" and is used less often than the other modes. The Locrian mode has a lowered 2nd, 3rd, 4th, 5th, 6th, and 7th scale degree of the Ionian mode (Benjamin et al., 1992; Ottman, 2004). It is acceptable to compose within the major or minor modes in modulating to a new tonic; mixing Dorian and Aeolian is common (Benjamin et al., 1992).

The Doctrine of Affections was based on the philosophy that music can affect a person's character and behavior and that the different scales have different characteristics. Dorian is calming and easy to listen to. Phrygian makes people more passionate and able to inspire others, and Lydian causes weakness of the mind because of its simplicity (Jarboe, 2018).

Harding et al. (2023) listed songs that elicited specific emotional responses. Serenity, a positive valence with low arousal, was elicited by *Manoman's Meditation*. Listening to Vivaldi's Four Seasons: Spring, a positive valence with high arousal, elicited joy. Sadness, a negative valence with low arousal, was elicited with Beethoven's *Moonlight Sonata*. Fear, a negative valence with high arousal, resulted when listening to Mussorgsky's *Night on Bald Mountain*.

An effect is a state of mind and body related to feelings or emotions (Jarboe, 2018). The body would stay in one affection unless acted on by a stimulus. The stimulus moves the effect, and then the effect informs your mind of the emotion you are feeling. Examples of arousing emotions have been documented in 1739 by Johann Matheson in *The Perfect Chapelmaster*. One example is using different intervals; large intervals facilitate joy, while small intervals facilitate sadness. The use of rapid rhythmic patterns facilitates feelings of anger (Jarboe, 2018). Bensimon (2020) discussed the use of rhythms as relating to motivation. Hakvoort et al. (2020) discussed the uses of rhythm in music during music therapy. Jarboe (2018) lists the major and minor key signatures and their corresponding associated moods and feelings.

Compositionally, it is an accepted practice to modulate up or down, to change key, by a perfect 4th or a perfect 5th, comfortable intervals. The onset of 20th-century music forms, such as 12-tone, tetra chord-based compositional styles and minimalism, afford composers/artists additional methods that evolved from the traditional baroque, classical, and romantic eras. Musical expression has become more complex and still links to conventional methods, developing side by side during the latter half of the 20th century, expanding popular music (Benjamin et al., 1992; Kennan & Grantham, 1997; Ottman, 2004).

Traditional music analysis reveals key tonalities and structure. Schenkerian analysis reveals patterns within the structure, such as rhythms, tonality, etc. (Wadsworth, 2016). Combining both analysis techniques can illustrate what selections work for different effects of PTSD and why they work. The research has been done on specific composers and their works, as published score anthologies, such as the Norton Critical Score Series, are commonly available for score study. Research was not widely found as to what different aspects of music are effective in addressing specific PTSD effects.

Duman (2023) discussed sound frequencies, music, and human perception, focusing on the debate about the tuning standard used in music. Theorists believe that 432 Hz corresponds to specific harmonics associated with the golden ratio and the Schumann resonances in a particular relationship to the musical note A4. The researchers stated that 432 Hz positively affects the chakras and accelerates our spiritual growth, that 432 Hz is an awakening, an opening of the heart center, of love, harmony, and joy, and is sometimes referred to as the frequency of the universe. Listening to music tuned to 432 Hz can create a sense of comfort and relaxation (Duman, 2023).

As determined by NASA, the Schumann resonance is 8 Hz. 8 Hz, as a submultiple of 432 Hz, is the mathematical base for the relationship between frequency and octave music (Duman, 2023). Utilizing the 432 Hz tuning means that the musical note A4, in the center piano octave, is tuned to 432 Hz. Listening to music tuned to A = 432 Hz can create a more harmonious and relaxing experience and is believed to resonate with the human body and alignment with nature (Duman, 2023).

Duman (2023) concluded that since the cosmos is composed of matter that vibrates at various frequencies, including humans, it is clear that sound is a basic function. Sound promotes healing and boosts one's well-being since sound can affect our mental and physical states. Historical events influenced by numerous social and political factors and commercial interests can be used to explain how A = 440 Hz came to be employed over A = 432 Hz as the standard tuning frequency (Duman, 2023).

In researching "EMO music," Google Scholar did not produce relevant results, in my opinion. When searching using the search bar, several video examples, other closely related searches, and a link to Wikipedia showcasing a definition of Emo as a music genre, providing a history and developments of the genre, and numerous musical examples from the beginning in the 1980s to the present.

The link is https://en.wikipedia.org/wiki/Emo.

Emo music is characterized by emotion and describes any music that expresses emotion. It often has confessional lyrics, also known as emotional hardcover or emocore. Emo originated in hardcore punk and is considered a genre of alternative rock, punk rock, and pop punk. Some examples include characteristics of progressive rock, such as complex guitar work, nontraditional song forms or structures, and extreme range or shifts in dynamics (Wikipedia contributors, 2024). Many of these musical characteristics are found in Romantic-era music and were discussed earlier.

Emo lyrics, often confessional, are typically emotional and deal with topics such as failed romance, pain, insecurity, suicidal thoughts, love, and relationships. Early Emo bands differed from the aggression, anger, and traditional verse-chorus-verse form structure or hardcover punk. Emo also signifies the relationship between fans and artists and aspects of fashion, culture, and behavior (Wikipedia contributors, 2024).

Chapter 10

Discoveries: My Research

As you can tell, I found information on and researched music-based support systems emphasizing music and brotherhood. Mrs. Jennifer Parrish, MA, BCBA, LBA, has reviewed the information contained within this manuscript, chapters 9 and 10, for data accuracy and interpretation and to ensure the removal of researcher bias. The Abstract, presented in an article form, would appear before the introduction and background inform-ation. For presentation in this book, it is being set in this position. Here is what I discovered during my research.

Abstract

Veterans can experience the effect of their PTSD outside of a clinical setting and may turn to a comfort-able method of addressing their self-care, such as listening to music. The problem addressed by this study was that veterans often experience PTSD incidents but are not aware of what measures they may take to employ a music therapy-based self-care regimen to address the specific effect of PTSD, especially when outside of a clinical setting. The researcher did not find literature that specifically addressed music therapy and the particular effects of PTSD; some assumptions were transferred from general studies about music therapy and studies about PTSD due to a lack of specifically related literature available. This study used a survey method to gather information from licensed clinicians and veterans on music selections addressing the effects of PTSD. A qualitative analysis was chosen for this study, and an interpretive phenomenological analysis was finally selected. Clinicians will be able to exchange information on music repertoire and add to their treatment music selections, overall as well as by specific effects; veterans will be able to see what their peers are employing for "self-care" when the need arises outside of a clinical setting and add to their treatment regimen. Research has found an increase in the employment of a music therapy-based treatment plan to facilitate quality of life; however, several gaps were identified, including a lack of specificity in reporting. This study adds specificity to the research by showing the top selections employed by clinicians, veterans, and overall in addressing PTSD.

Keywords: PTSD, music therapy, self-care

Problem Statement

The problem addressed by this study was that veterans often experience PTSD incidents but are not aware of what measures they may take to employ a music therapy-based self-care regimen to address the specific effect of PTSD, especially when outside of a clinical setting, which will meet their needs. The researcher did not find literature that specifically addressed music therapy and the specific effects of PTSD; some assumptions are transferred from general studies about music therapy and PTSD due to a lack of subject-specific related literature available.

Often, veterans can sense the warning signs of an upcoming PTSD incident, but not always. Veterans can experience PTSD incidents anywhere; it all depends on what their trigger is. Many incidents are triggered visually, such as sudden bright flashes of light, or from seeing an event like what was experienced, such as a small structure fire in an outdoor setting, or seeing the aftermath of a nature event, which can bring back a memory. Audio stimulation is also common in facilitating a PTSD incident. Often, this takes on the form of an audio file, a sound bite of a film, or other visual or projected media of an event, frequently found on social media or YouTube (Hammond, 2017; Mayo Clinic, 2022). Loud, unexpected bangs, pops, or even rapid-sounding pops may sound like gunfire or an explosive device. Presentations on the Tet Offensive from the Vietnam War, the liberation of Kuwait, or Operation Desert Shield/Desert Storm I can be a powerful facilitator to a PTSD event, particularly at times such as the anniversary of these or other operations or significant historical events, such as the Oklahoma City bombing on 19 Apr 95, or the loss of the USS Challenger, 28 Jan 86. A veteran seeing oneself in a visual presentation is quite a powerful trigger. Sensitivity to sound, light, and hyperawareness are some of the results of PTSD (Hammond, 2017; Mayo Clinic, 2022). Knowing what they can listen to so that they may address the effects of PTSD can be a valuable resource for veterans.

Purpose of the Study

The purpose of this study was to raise awareness of what listening to music, some of which may be found on a smartphone or other mobile device, as an option for addressing different effects of PTSD; specific-ally, what music selections are being employed to address the effects of PTSD. This study allowed clinicians and veterans to exchange information among and between veterans and be informative to clinicians. Specifically, who can benefit from the different selections and how they may benefit from their selections. Clinicians will be able to apply specific music repertoire and add to their treatment music selections overall for PTSD, as well as by specific PTSD effects. They can add selections that are not currently employed as a treatment option. Clinicians can learn what veterans are listening to for the different effects of PTSD and can add those selections to their treatment repertoire. Veterans can see what their peers employ for self-care (songs or genres listed for each effect of PTSD) when the need arises outside of a clinical setting (basically, in life when not at an appointment) and can add music selections to their self-care treatment regimen. Veterans will learn what other veterans are employing to address the effects of PTSD and have additional resources available to choose from. The two stakeholders can exchange information and add to their treatment music repertoire, facilitating an efficient option for addressing the specific effects of PTSD. This information may also help non-veterans with PTSD in addressing their needs.

What do veterans listen to for self-treating the effects of PTSD? Does the genre/style of music, the composer/artist, and the specific song title(s) matter? What music (breakdown: style/genre, artists/composers, most often used song titles) is listened to for what effect (list each effect and top music selections)? Does the tonal key or mode matter in selections? What do clinicians utilize in their employment of music-based self-therapy for PTSD? Are there specific songs, artists, styles, etc., that are employed more often in the treatment of the effects of PTSD? These questions will be investigated to discover what is being used and whether styles or other musical elements had a bearing on the effectiveness of music selections for addressing the effects of PTSD. This information facilitated addressing specific effects of PTSD.

Significance of the study

In assembling literature for this study, the researcher discovered that existing literature that addresses music therapy and PTSD, or specifically the effects of PTSD, was not commonly available. This study focused on a specific aspect of music therapy and addressed the effects of PTSD. The need for more research and specificity in that research was a commonly found theme in the literature available. This study contributed to the available research by adding some of the specificity sought by the available literature.

Information from this study could be employed by veterans while engaging in a self-care regimen when not in a clinical setting. Listening to music, as part of the music therapy treatment plan, can alter moods and is well documented as a treatment method for PTSD overall. Veterans will have additional music selections with which to address their specific effects of PTSD; this information is not commonly available outside of a clinical setting unless spread socially by word-of-mouth, by recommendations from support groups, or directly from friends.

Gooding and Langston (2019) conducted a scoping review of music therapy with military populations. This review found an increase in the employment of a music therapy-based treatment plan to facilitate quality of life;

however, several gaps were identified, including a need for more specificity in reporting. Music selections employed for the different effects of PTSD are one type of specificity that veterans and clinicians can utilize in choosing music sections for a self-care regimen.

Gathering data from veterans provided information from those employing a music therapy-based approach to addressing the effects of PTSD, both in a clinical setting and in a self-care setting. Providing details on addressing a specific effect of PTSD and its corresponding musical selection(s) raises awareness of one type of support available for PTSD.

Conceptual Framework

This study focused on the availability of and the importance of PTSD support, specifically music therapy, and the specific effects of PTSD. It prepared the groundwork for future research into music's effectiveness in addressing the effects of PTSD. The study focused on the veterans to indicate known resources being employed and provide additional resources for the stakeholders. This study added to the foundation of research currently available, allowing future research to be built on this.

Support for PTSD could facilitate positive change in the quality of mental health and feelings of self-worth, socialization, and quality of life (Kirchner & Biniecki, S.

M. Y., 2019). This basic interpretation and line of thought led the researcher to the following conceptual framework:

Veteran + Support Services for PTSD = Life Success

This equation represents the path to achieving personal, professional, or academic success. Understanding what types of PTSD support are available and where said support is available facilitates academic success and translates to life success (De Los Santos et al., 2019).

Method

This study had no ethical, consent, or conflict of interest concerns. The data retrieved by surveys will be stored and secured on a USB hard drive for three years. No participant or researcher received any compensation for this study. This study used a survey method to gather information on music selections addressing the effects of PTSD. Gathering data from the veteran's perspective was best accomplished in the surveys by also including open-ended discussion questions. The survey allowed the participants to expand on or elaborate on the different aspects of music, music therapy, and PTSD.

This study provided information on music selections that are often employed in treating specific effects of PTSD, thus building on the information available to veterans on addressing the effects of PTSD in a self-care setting. Song selections overall for PTSD and by specific

PTSD effect are listed in Tables 1-14; perspectives provided by the participants are discussed in the results section.

Participants completed a researcher-constructed survey for veterans. The survey was reviewed for clarity and to ensure the questions stayed within this study's goals. Later, the data, coding, analysis, and findings were reviewed to ensure accuracy and remove any researcher bias.

After the survey was reviewed, invitations were sent out to veterans with self-declared PTSD until a goal of 10 participants was reached. Invitations were sent via vetted veteran social media pages, such as on Facebook or LinkedIn, and by personal invitation from attending a veteran organization conference or other event.

The data was collected, sorted (overall and by PTSD effect), and input into an Excel sheet; then, it was analyzed for grouping by specific PTSD effect and for PTSD overall. The findings, the top three music selections overall for the study and the top three music selections by separate PTSD effect, as well as the descriptive analysis of music therapy as it relates to addressing specific effects of PTSD, were assembled into a data table for inclusion in the manuscript.

The researcher purchased the sheet music, or audio versions, for the selections listed on the tables to conduct a Schenkerian analysis, as applicable, and a traditional form analysis of the selections listed in the tables. Analysis was conducted, looking for common-alities among each effect's selections (tone, mode, composer, title, etc.). Commonalities and other informa-tion were included in the manuscript. This information was then reviewed to ensure the accuracy of the data and the interpretation of the findings and to remove any researcher bias. Tables 1-14 list the study's overall PTSD results and each specific PTSD effect. All data collected, all surveys received, and the resulting Excel sheets will be kept on an external secure USB hard drive for three years and then destroyed.

Sample

An invitation was sent via social media outlets, using professional pages, not personal pages, to veteran-related organizations' pages targeting veterans with self-reported PTSD until a population of 10 veterans with self-reported PTSD responded. This sample was obtained by an online invitation via LinkedIn and Facebook vetted veterans' organizations and group pages.

The participant number was based on the postal abbre-viation for the state to which the participant sent the response; the prefix number is the number of responses received from that state, and the suffix number is the number of responses received from that specific town/city. A one-letter designator was added to the end of the sequence to notate responses from a veteran or a clinician, represented by a "V" for the veteran and a "C" for the clinician; for example, 02-TN-05-V is for the second response from TN and the fifth response from that city/town and is from a veteran. Demographic information, the branch of service of the participants, is shown in Figure 1.

Basic Music Form Analysis and Schenkerian Analysis

A fundamental understanding of basic music theory and form structures is necessary to analyze music. Skills such as these are often taught as music fundamentals: the ability to recognize key signatures, basic triads and chord structures, chord progressions and how they relate to establishing a tonal center, often a major or minor key, and a recognition of the classical and 20th-century music forms (sonata, ABA, diatonic modes/the church modes, pentatonic, whole tone, 12-tone) (Benjamin et al., 1992; Ottman, 2004).

In music therapy, music is employed to enhance an individual's state of being; often, this requires a coping mechanism to facilitate the alteration or cancellation of an undesired mood or emotion (Ophir & Jacoby, 2020). Music has been associated with moods, most often with either being happy or sad; the Ionian mode is happy, the most common of the major tonalities, and Aeolian is sad, the most common of the minor tonalities (Benjamin et al., 1992).

The researcher conducted two musical analysis methods to further seek commonalities among the selections for addressing different effects. The traditional classical analysis looks at the music from the bottom up, chord by chord or beat by beat, which determines the progression horizontally. The Schenkerian analysis is like the traditional method in looking at the chords and music structure from the bottom up; however, it looks at the music and structure in layers and larger-scale shapes and patterns as the music moves horizontally; it is also partially an auditory analysis (Benjamin et al., 1992; Ottman, 2004; Wadsworth, 2016). Different analysis methodologies provided different perspectives on how to approach the data analysis.

Instrument and Design

To provide information most effectively on what is being employed for addressing the different effects of PTSD, specific perceptions from the veterans had to be considered. Participants were provided with the opportunity to list their top three selections for the various effects of PTSD and for addressing PTSD overall and to differentiate when one musical selection worked in this one case but not in a different case. Their perspective added context and meaning to the musical options, as well as the how and why needed to be able to be expressed and understood.

A qualitative analysis was chosen for this study, and an interpretive phenomenological analysis (IPA) was finally selected. The participants stated their music selections overall for PTSD and, by separating PTSD effects, how they employ music therapy techniques. The participants also provided a textual description of their perspective on music therapy, the benefits, and any other information about how they use music therapy methods and/or how the experience happens, as well as what they felt while applying the music intervention. Utilizing the participant's direct quotes, an IPA approach will convey the participant's perceptions of an experience, employing music, or music therapy, to address the effects of PTSD and will allow for portraying the complexities of music and mood/emotion (Creswell, 2013; Moustakas, 1994; Ophir & Jacoby, 2020).

The researcher-constructed survey was explicitly designed to address the effects of PTSD and the veteran's perceptions. After the data was collected, the researcher conducted a traditional music form analysis and a Schenkerian analysis, when appropriate, of the most common music selections (overall in the survey and by specific PTSD effect) to determine commonalities of tonal key, structure, rhythm, or other music attribute, and their emotions and/or PTSD effect. The survey included identifying music selections and sections for the participants to provide their perceptions of music therapy in addressing PTSD.

Results

The researcher has experienced the phenomenon of music addressing the effects of PTSD; as a veteran and as a music performer, this was a natural outlet. Different music selections sometimes worked for the same effect, but the surrounding environments differed. The researcher would listen to Copland's *Fanfare for the Common Man* to gain focus, calm, and motivation. By the end, the researcher often found himself conducting; other times, the researcher would be fingering the 1st Horn part from muscle memory as it played (the final note, a concert D, was always best in tune when fingered T-3). That last chord instilled feelings of accomplishments from the past and of what is yet to come. Other times, the Beatles' *Here Comes the Sun* or *Let It Be* would elicit feelings of calm and focus and provide a different sense of motivation. When employing Frank Zappa as a musical inspiration, the researcher has also felt a different type of calm, often a tiny smile and a feeling of moving forward. Music does not always have the same effect on everyone; it frequently depends on the context of the situation. What follows is a discussion from veterans' perspectives on their experiences with music to address the effects of PTSD.

Findings

This narrative provides a comprehensive guide to music preferences and their effects on various PTSD symptoms for veterans. Of the six participants, five were in the US Army, and one was in the US Navy. The bold double-slash separates the participants' responses. The top three music selections listed for addressing PTSD were:

1. Ambient Instrument-Waterscapes//*Adagio for Strings*, Samuel Barber//432 Hz music, no words//Alternative Rock// "Waterscapes (beach or rainforest)"//*Fire in My Head*, Two Feet.

2. Rock or Alternative//*Appalachian Spring Suit*, Aaron Copeland//Alternative or Heavy Metal, Disturbed//Hip-Hop//Water Life, Whales no seagulls//*Friends and Strangers*, Ronnie Laws.

3. Praise and Worship//Soca, specific reggae Bob Marley, steel pan sounds found in Trinidad and Tobago//*Nessun Dorma*, Puccini//Lo-fi/Instrumental//Folk-pop, Noah Kahan or Taylor Swift//*Principles of Lust: Sadness, Finding Love, Sadness* (Reprise). See Table 1.

Tables 2-14 list the top three selections by specific effect. Only one respondent provided particular songs for the Top 3 Selections by PTSD Effect. The other respondents provided comments, selections, or genres listed in no specific order. Here is the "Top-3" selection list for addressing PTSD effects. For Hyperawareness: a. *Alesia* by Eluveitie, b. *BYOB* by System of a Down, c. *Chasm* by Flyleaf. For Depression: a. *Bro Hymn* by Pennywise, b. *How Great Thou Art*, c. *Morning Has Broken* by John Denver. For Anger: a. *Blut Im Auge* by Equilibrium, b. *Na Na Na* by My Chemical Romance, c. *Zombified* by Falling in Reverse. For Insomnia: a. *River Flows in You* (Yiruma) b. *Autumn* by Antonio Vivaldi, c. *Tamarack Pines* by George Winston. For Fear of Crowds: a. DMX (almost all songs), b. *I'm Shipping Up to Boston*, by Dropkick Murphys, c. select Metallica/Beastie Boys songs "that put me in more of a fight (if necessary) than flight mode." No specific songs were listed for Isolationism, Poor Concentration, or Mood Swings.

The participants' comments regarding genres and sounds provided, listed as stated by the participants to be in no particular order, follow. Comments on hyperawareness are listed as listening to alternative/heavy metal, such as the group Disturbed. One respondent said, "Nothing, I fully concentrate on my surroundings." Comments for depression were listed as *TN Whiskey* by Chris Stapleton, *Take Me Home Country Roads* by John Denver, and *Oohh Child* by Five Stair Steps. Another respondent listed *Adagio for Strings* by Samuel Barber "for a good cry" or *Here Comes the Sun* by the Beatles "to lift my mood." One respondent listed hip-hop as their choice of listening, while another listed 432 Hz music. Isolationism comments: listening to a "wide variety, no Techno or Punk-Rock or Heavy Metal," Learning new guitar pieces (e.g., *Big Love* by Lindsey Buckingham), and Folk-pop such as Noah Kahan or Taylor Swift. Comments for poor concentration were Trance and 432 Hz music. Comments for mood swings were Folk-pop artists such as Noah Kahan or Taylor Swift. One respondent would "do the same as below (anger) given the opportunity." For Anger, one respondent listed a "variety of Peloton work-out hip-hop. Another respondent listed silence and reflection, while another listed 432 Hz music. One respondent listed rock music as their choice. For insomnia, one respondent listed waterscapes/water life from Amazon. Another respondent listed a "thunderstorm sound generator, hopefully with Alpha waves, while another listed 432 Hz music. For flashback, one respondent said, "I avoid all types of sounds." Another listed 432 Hz music. For anxiety, one respondent said, "I sing hymns rather than listen to music for acute anxiety." One respondent combined music selections from hyperaware-ness and mood swings. Another respondent listens to country storytelling songs such as *In Color*, *Come and Get Higher*, and *Remember When*. Other respondents listed Lo-fi/Instrumental and 432 Hz music. For memory loss, one respondent said, "I just keep to myself and try to remember the topic or try to forget the look on people's faces when I forget well-known or simple-to-remember historical information." Another respondent listed 432 Hz music. For fear of crowds, one respondent listed Alternative/Heavy Metal such as Disturbed.

When asked about triggers having a bearing on music preference, responses varied. Participant 01-VA-01-V stated that "other selections work, provided that they have the same intensity needed. Anger and anxiety, I can't calm down until I unload 'excess energy' (respondent's quotation marks) and then can switch to something more peaceful." Participant 01-CT-01-V stated that they tend to pick genres of music to listen to, such as Baroque, Country, Hard Rock, etc. "I have never consciously used music as a therapy modality and find it terribly difficult to complete section 4 (list by specific effect) without some help." Participant 01-TN-01-V stated, "I do end up slowly swop genres." Participant 01-NC-01-V said, "I have noticed that music can heavily influence my mood, but how I feel prior to listening to music will determine whether the same song positively or negatively impacts how I feel while listening and after listening to the selected music. I must be in a very positive mental space in order to listen to anything with vocals, so I depend heavily on 432Hz Music for the most negative symptoms, feelings, and moments." Participant

01-VA-01-V stated, "Absolutely, and just in the same way a movie/show selection does. I refrain at home (or anywhere) from watching war movies, and I refrain at work or home from listening to anything that will trigger me or heighten my anxiety/reaction." Participant 02-TN-02-V stated that the three selections listed in question three (Two Feet's *Fire in My Head*, Ronnie Law's *Friends and Strangers*, and Enigma's *Principles of Lust*) are their primary selections for all their triggers.

When discussing MusiCorps and other similar organizations, five respondents did not know of such organizations, and one did. Participant 01-TN-01-V mentioned Guitar for Vets and VA Whole Health Music Therapy.

When asked to provide additional information on music, music therapy, PTSD, and any other information that the participant felt should be mentioned and included in this study, participants provided specific and individualized information. Participant 01-CT-01-V shared, "I am a singer and a guitarist. When it comes to music, I look for music I can perform and take full advantage of my voice and my prowess on the acoustic guitar. For the last 10 years, it's been the only way I have been able to express emotion. When listening to music, I tend to pick genres and not particular songs." Participant 01-TN-01-V stated, "[music is] helpful to ID my feelings both before and during music." Participant 01-NC-01-V said, "The 432Hz frequency music has been one of the most effective tools that I have used to manage symptoms. I incorporate it into breathing exercises, meditation with biofeedback, and journaling exercises to explore mood and the impact before and after the exercise, a 2 to 5-minute pause to listen to the frequency music and do some mindfulness breathing exercises and return to journaling using writing prompts such as the following: i. Once your mind is clear, write down the first few things that you think of. ii. Write about something peaceful and serene." Participant 01-VA-01-V stated, "I have never used music as a form of clinical treatment and have only just used music for the time and purpose that I need for." Participant 02-TN-02-V said, "My triggers/situations often require more of a genre approach than an individual song selection. When I am feeling depressed, I listen to my playlist labeled "Upbeat," which consists of [the] upbeat R&B genre. Hyper-awareness, anger, anxiety, mood swings, and flashbacks, I listen to my playlist "Nice," which is comprised of contemporary jazz, alternative/indie, and classic soul. These are the most notable PTSD triggers I find myself in a constant struggle with. Listening to music within these genres helps my mind slow down, reflect, analyze, and make better plans, hopefully, to produce more favorable outcomes."

Evaluation of the Findings

The data received indicated that listing specific music titles for addressing PTSD was not easy for five out of six of the participants. Participants stated that addressing PTSD or its effects is more of a genre approach than using specific music selections. A few themes appeared from the data; however, data saturation still needed to be reached. There were six different "Top 3" lists for addressing PTSD (overall), one for each participant. The participants' selections included jazz, nature sounds, classical vocal and instrumental music, new-age music, and American pop/hip-hop. One theme, a classical music selection, was listed as a top one, a top two, and a top three tier. A second theme of Waterscapes/ Water Life appeared as a tier one and two response. The third theme, instrumental music, was listed as a tier one and tier three response. The fourth theme, New Age/ Alternative Rock, appeared as a tier two and a tier three response. Specifically, 432 Hz music, rock, Hip-Hop, Heavy Metal, Praise and Worship, ambient music, American singer-songwriter, Lo-Fi, New Age music, and Reggae were each listed once as a "Top-3" selection or genre. Water and nature sounds were listed twice, while water and ambient music were listed once. Alternative rock music was listed three times, once in tier one and twice in tier two. See Table 1. Music perception research has identified the role of specific musical structures, such as tonality, timbre, and tempo, in music-evoked emotional responses (Bronson et al., 2018). Clinical evidence supports that relaxation music can help with coping and psychological transitioning after release from the ICU (Pant et al., 2022). Music is used to either enhance or change one's mood (Peters et al., 2023).

When discussing the 13 effects of PTSD individually, 432 Hz music was mentioned seven times; Rock music and Folk Pop music as a genre or as the song selection style were each listed five times; Hip-Hop and Heavy Metal as a genre or as the song selection style were each mentioned four times; Alternative Rock, by genre or as the song selection style was listed three times; water and nature sounds, praise and worship music or spirituals by genre or as the song selection style was listed two times; ambient music, Folk Metal (Swiss, German) music and solo-piano music as a genre or as the song selection style were each listed two times. As a genre or song selection style, American singer-songwriters, Lo-fi music, New Age music, classical music, American Country, Soul music, and Celtic Rock were mentioned once. See Tables 2-14. This variety of music genres utilized by the participants indicates the numerous and various selections available that were effective for addressing the PTSD effects. Music that is effective for addressing PTSD is individualized to meet the individual veteran's needs. Music therapy can be effective as a treatment tool for psychological conditions, and more research is needed in this area (Echezona, 2023; Thomas &

Chichaya, 2023). Future research may focus on the psychological effects of different styles of music (Huang & Li, 2022; Thomas & Chichaya, 2023).

Discussion

Music therapy has been well-documented and discussed (chapters 9 and 10 of this book) as a treatment tool for clinicians to employ when addressing PTSD. The resources available in the literature discussed (chapters 9 and 10 of this book) are goal-oriented but not specific to the tools to be used; genres and types of music and sounds are discussed, but only some particular music selections are discussed. The literature indicated that such specificity was needed. Veterans and clinicians will benefit from the results and findings of this study.

There was a repetition of a few data points of the top three selections for PTSD overall; however, data saturation was not reached. Numerous participants, five out of the six, listed their selections "in no particular order" when discussing the listed effects of PTSD. The open discussion questions also reflected this difficulty in ranking their music selections for specific effects. The participants mentioned that there were times when different selections were employed for the same effect. Still, they were either in various settings or the desired emotional outcome differed for that occasion. The time and place of "treatment" sometimes dictated the selection from a list. The participants' comments and observations reflect the data available in the literature.

One limitation of this study was the small sample size— six respondents —and the fact that only two services were represented, the Army (5) and the Navy (1). A more significant number of participants and participants representing more of the military services would provide a broader scope for collecting data and providing further information.

Implications for Practice

This study added specificity to the literature regarding music for addressing PTSD and reflected available information from the literature that various genres of music elicit specific emotional outcomes. The information revealed in the analysis can be shared among the stakeholders (veterans and clinicians) during a group setting, during a 1:1 Peer Intervention, or daily as part of a daily routine to efficiently exchange information and ideas that can be included in a treatment plan or can be exchanged within the veteran's support systems. The breakdown by genre can be employed to construct playlists. The specific music selections discussed can be shared, possibly providing additional resources for addressing PTSD.

Recommendations

The researcher recommends that further studies be conducted to list specific songs/genres to address PTSD and its particular effects. A database can be established listing music/genres for PTSD overall and for its various effects. Eventually, the database will be used to construct playlists for veterans. Playlists can be effect-specific or for PTSD in general. The therapeutic effects of various genres have not received enough attention in the available research (Huang & Li, 2022).

A study can be conducted to find out why music selections/genres are effective in addressing PTSD or its effects. Employing a traditional form analysis and a Shakarian analysis can identify the commonalities of the effective selections. Is it a consistent divided beat, or could a rhythmic or melodic ostinato be the common element? Is it the tonality or the mode? More research is needed in this area (Echezona, 2023; Peters et al., 2023; Thomas & Chichaya, 2023).

Once these elements are identified, music can be composed to address PTSD or a specific effect. Music therapists can employ a musical composition element in the treatment plan that can tailor the new music to a particular effect or PTSD overall. Such music therapy can be an effective tool to address psychological conditions such as PTSD (Echezona, 2023).

Conclusion

How music affects the brain is well documented. However, "why" may not be clearly understood. The neurological and physiological effects are well documented. However, what facilitates those reactions? Research into the "how" and "why" of music and its effectiveness in addressing PTSD is in its infancy. More research in this area is needed to discover and offer more or different musical options for addressing PTSD on an individual basis or as part of a treatment plan. Music's therapeutic effects on a person's mood, thoughts, feelings, and outlook on life and self are essential for the veteran. Music can heal.

Chapter 11

Intimate Discoveries - A Quick Thought or Two

One's state of mind influences one's academic journey; this was the case for me. Starting as a veteran with issues of my own was not the best frame of mind to start being educational, and the combination of my divorce and transitioning to the civilian world were major mental distractions. I was climbing my way out of the hole I was in. I have already talked about support from fellow students and my fraternity, but now I want to turn things inward to the value of support from music.

I had much support at Cameron University and the University of Oklahoma, as was already shared. My relationships with my fellow students, especially with my Brothers and Sisters of Kappa Kappa Psi and Tau Beta Sigma, were phenomenal. I also had some great relationships with my professors, and I needed it one time in particular. It was on the day of the final, and I missed it; I covered that story in my previous book about my academic journey.

During my doctoral journey, I was still single with no family around for several hundreds of miles, and I only had a minimal support system. I had very few friends, and only one or two were veterans. About a year into my doctoral program, I moved to Tennessee with the hopes of employment as a music teacher. It didn't work out; I was too expensive for the schools, so I became a substitute teacher. After a school year and a half, I resigned when "get off YouTube and back on Google Classroom" was a common utterance. I was a babysitter, not a teacher. I eventually found other jobs.

My other employment was as a Wal-Mart Fuel Attendant at a fuel center by my house. I have a small circle of friends from work who were a support system, and I even taught some of them when I was a substitute teacher.

Okay, now you know where I got my support from and the various segments of my life. What I would like to talk about now is that one of the most constant PTSD support systems for me has been music. I guess this is no surprise. I've used music to relieve the effects of PTSD, motivate me, and improve my quality of life and myself.

I cannot stress the importance of a positive emotional and mental outlook on my academic success. When I was down, so was my academic performance. When I was up, things rocked! The source for a core support group or support system does not matter; the connection with your support group or your support system needs to be meaningful to you. I love music.

Picture 13:
Peter Burke, CU Pep rally, circa 2010-2011.

Between moving to MO and beginning my doctoral journey, I slipped away from my music. I still listened, but I no longer composed. My playing time was limited. I felt like playing only sometimes. It reached the point where I would take out my Horn and play some warm-up long tones or short passages, and I needed more motivation to play.

I was in TN when I sold my Horn. Yes, I sold my Horn, which has been all over the world with me. I did not want to let it go. Unfortunately, I needed to eat and pay my bills, so the Horn was sold. I wasn't totally without an ax. I had been given a Horn that belonged to a friend of mine at OU. Their parents sent me the Horn because of my appreciation of the Horn; it's fantastic, and due to the relationship that MB and I had. I was a mentor. They were a dear friend of mine.

I have to say that I have cherished my new Horn and the memories that MB and I share. I can hold it and feel comfort. I don't have to play it; just keeping it as if I were to play it gives me peace. I have dabbled with it from time to time. I haven't performed in an ensemble yet. But I will.

I found the SVA while finishing my doctorate. Eventually, I found the Xi Eta chapter of Kappa Kappa Psi at Austin Peay State University. I found them in the fall semester of 2024. They became a chapter on 27 April 2024, in the spring semester of 2024.

I went to a few concerts, and after the first concert, I joined the Hymn Circle and Shout Out. I stayed outside the circle since no one knew me, but they saw my KKY hat. I invited myself to sing. I met and chatted with a few chapter members and their advisers. For the next concert, I was approached and welcomed. I was asked to participate actively in the Hymn Circle and give the Shout-out! Well, needless to say, I felt very much at home. Oh, by the way, both concerts ROCKED!

So, this year, I have made it a point to stay active in the SVA. I am affiliated with the Legion in the area; the SVA and the Legion did a joint service project. I have made it a point to have an affiliation with the Xi Eta chapter of Kappa Kappa Psi. I'll be attending concerts as often as possible and supporting them at the Veterans Football game and other events around the community. I have acquired a new sense of hope; Kappa Kappa Psi will do that. I will slowly get back into the music scene. I'd love to be a guest conductor or give a few master's Classes! We will see.

Chapter 12

An After Thought: Me and the Grand Ole Opry

This part could have been more comfortable for me to write. I will be talking about the highs and the lows of my experiences that night, Friday, 5 Jan 2024. I remember being excited and looking forward to going to the Opry! It was a Friday evening, and I was going to my room to pick up a jacket for the night. It would only be in the 30s that night when the show would be over, so I wanted to be prepared. Well, I got to my room and was locked out! This wouldn't have bothered me, except it was the second time that day.

Earlier, one of the housekeepers had to inform the front desk that I was not checked out and was still staying for the weekend. I was lucky they were in the hall then to help with my room. Yes, this is the short version of this. I was assured everything was fine, so I went out for my afternoon sessions. When I returned to get ready for the evening, that's when things went sour.

I arrived at my room and tried to use my key card to enter my room. I placed the card against the reader and heard a slight hum, but the light didn't change, and there was no click. I was locked out. So. Anxiety rising, I pulled out my cell phone and called the front desk. After being told that security would be there in about 30 to 45 minutes, I decided to walk the 5 minutes to one of the shops. So, I walked. I found a long-sleeved, zip-up, sweater-type thing. It was black, warm, and, most of all, available. Available now. So, I now had an outer garment to wear to the Opry Hall.

I would be warm walking from the convention center and hotel to the Opry Hall, about a five or 6-minute walk from door to door. Anyway, I was anxious as I walked and figured I'd better buy something to wear back to my room. As I said, it would be in the lower 30s, and I wanted to be prepared. I was distracted by thinking about needing a coat as an outer garment and the chill. I should have taken a few more exterior pictures, but I had difficulty taking a clear picture; they were often blurry. Nerves, anxiety, or cold all contributed to the shakes. So, I did get a few shots, but not many.

I entered the venue and went immediately to the shop. I bought myself a dark gray hoodie! It's comfortable. I knew I'd be OK for the walk back. I explored the site once I knew I'd be OK for the walk back. I found my section and seat location and went up. My anticipation was growing. I couldn't believe I was in the mecca of country music venues; you're not Country Music Hall of Fame caliber unless you've performed in "The Circle."

I found my seat in the penultimate row from the top. It was quite a steep angle up to my seat, but the view was phenomenal! The view and the crowd, coupled with my previous experience that evening, gave me a bit of anxiety. I felt anxious, but at the same time, I was excited to be there. I found myself engaging in a self-soothing behavior; I found myself rocking. It wasn't much, but enough, something I don't remember doing in years.

I also found myself fortunate. Those around me were student-veterans. Those around me understood about anxiety. I didn't feel like it was being held against me. My anxiety went up and down but lessened in intensity as the night went on. I noticed that there were times when I wasn't rocking! I was definitely affected by my environment, by those around me, and by the music. Due to the subject matter, I noticed times when memories rolled down my cheek. It was country music, after all. Memories of people no longer with us, memories of places visited long ago and of the deeds done, and memories of people I've lost contact with; yes, even of old trucks and dogs. I loved every minute of it! The music touched me in my heart and my mind. I was having a wonderful time; however, I felt a bit anxious when the concert ended, so I gracefully exited the lobby as fast as possible. Once in the lobby, I took a few deep breaths before heading outside, walking a little slower than before, yet efficiently. Once I was outside, I felt better and not as anxious. During the walk back to the hotel, I was warm! That felt good. I like my new hoodie! I felt a lot better after the concert than I was feeling beforehand.

At the concert, I had people sitting behind me and in front of me, but no one was next to me in the same row I was sitting in. I think part of my anxiety was the fact that amid the crowd, I was by myself. I would have felt better and not been as anxious if I had shared the event and the experience with someone. I must have looked strange talking to myself while taking pictures or just commenting out loud; *you're missing a great show* to no one in particular.

I regret not taking more pictures, especially of the exterior. I did take a few, but they were a little blurry. I was calming down a little—after all, I had a plan during my walk to the concert—but I was feeling a little chill. With some of the lighting, it may have taken a pretty cool picture with a little blur. I'll have to see what pictures I have saved. I do have some cool videos.

Music is very therapeutic. It is relaxing, motivating, and emotional in so many ways. I loved my time at the Grand Ole Opry! I was with student-veterans mixed in among the crowd. I was with my Brothers and Sisters. Although I was in excellent company, the music carried me through what could have been a negative experience. I found comfort in the music.

Picture 14:
Peter Burke, NatCon 2024.

Chapter 13

Concluding Thoughts

As a student-veteran, I observed that higher education, in many respects, is an extension of a military career— you continue to explore and learn. Your world is expanded, relationships are formed, and networks are established. Your "social media" circle will not only include veterans from your past but will grow and expand as your academic journey develops.

Military training and 'way of life' never wholly leave us; our memories and experiences make us who we are, and they will always be a part of us. I have found that the strongest bonds I have formed with others in higher education, with other students or faculty, have been when there is complete acceptance and honesty between individuals. Some of my best memories involve activities and bonds with my Brothers of Kappa Kappa Psi and Sisters of Tau Beta Sigma. I found a family of fellow instrumental musicians; they were beginning their musical journey while I had been on mine for over 30 years already. Our shared experiences, opportunities, and stories have built relationships that will stand for time; we are Brothers.

One does not accomplish things and succeeds alone. Trying to do so would be a lonely and challenging academic journey.

Picture 15:
Peter Burke, my view, 15 Sep 2009.

References

Baker, F. A., Metcalf, O., Varker, T., & O'Donnell, M. (2018). A systemic review of the efficacy of creative arts therapies in the treatment of adults with PTSD. *Psychological Trauma*: Theory, Research, Practice, and Policy, 10(6), 643-651. https://doi.org/10.1037/tra0000353.supp (Supplemental)

Benjamin, T., Horvit, M., & Nelson, R. (1992). Techniques and Materials of Tonal Music with an Introduction to Twentieth Century Techniques (4th edition). Belmont, CA: Wadsworth Publishing Company.

Bensimon, M. (2020). Perceptions of music therapists regarding their work with children living under continuous war threat: Experiential reframing of trauma through songs. *Nordic Journal of Music Therapy* (January 2020). https://doi.org/10.1080/08098131.2019.1703210

Bronson, H., Vaudreuil, R., & Bradt, J. (2018). Music therapy treatment of active-duty military: An overview of intensive outpatient and longitudinal care programs. *Music Therapy Perspectives*, 36(2), 195–206. https://doi.org/10.1093/mtp/miy006

Capezuti, E., Pain, K., Alamag, E., Chen, X. Q., Philbert, V., & Krieger, A. C. (2022). Systemic review: Auditory stimuli and sleep. *Journal of Clinical Sleep Medicine, 18*(6), 1697-1709. https://doi.ordoi0.5664/jcsm.9860

Creswell, J. W. (2013). *Qualitative Inquiry and Research Design: Choosing Among Five Approaches* (3rd ed). Thousand Oaks, CA: SAGE Publications.

De Los Santos, S. B., Kupczynski, L., & Mundy, M. A. (2019). Determining academic success in students with disabilities in higher education. *International Journal of Higher Education, 8*(2), 16–38. doi: 10.5430/ijhe.v8n2p16

Drozd, N. (2020). The therapeutic approach to military culture: A music therapist's perspective. *Journal of Medical Humanities, 2022*(43), 169-177.

Duman, N. (2023). Returning the universe: Examining the cosmic significance of sound frequencies, music and human perception. *Online Journal of Music Sciences, 8*(2), 160-171. https://doi.org/10.31811/ojomus.1395046

Echezona, G. N. (2023). A review on the effectiveness of music therapy for treatment of psychological conditions. *Journal of Education in Developing Areas (JEDA) Special Edition,* 32(2), 117-129. ISSN: 0189420X

Gooding, L. F., & Langston, D. G. (2019). Music Therapy with Military Populations: A Scoping Review. *Journal of Music Therapy*, 56(4), 315–347. https://doi.org/10.1093/jmt/thz010

Grout, D. (1980). A History of Western Music (3rd edition). New York, NY: Norton & Company.

Hakvoort, L., de Jong, S., van de Ree, M., Kok, T., Macfarlane, C., & de Haan, H. (2020). Music therapy to regulate arousal and attention in patients with substance use disorder and posttraumatic stress disorder: A feasibility study. *Journal of music therapy*, 57(3), 353-378. https://doi.org/10.1093/jmt/thaa007

Hammond, S. (2017). Student veterans in higher education: A conversation six decades in the making. *New Directions for Institutional Research, 2016* (171), 11–21. https://doi-org.proxy1.ncu.edu/10.1002/ir.20191

Harding, E. E., Gaudrain, E., Hrycyk, I. J., Harris, R. L., Tillman, B., Matt, B., Free, R. H., & Baskent, D. (2023). Musical emotion categorization with vocoders of varying temporal and spectral content. *Sounds in Hearing*, 27, 1-19. DOI: 10.1177/23312165221141142

Huang, J., & Li, X. (2022). Effects and applications of music therapy on psychological health: A review. *Advances in Social Science, Education and Humanities Research, 638*(ICPAHD 2021), 948-989. DOI: 10.2991/assehr.k.220110.186

Jarboe, K. E. (2018). The Doctrine of Affections: Emotion and Music. *The Research and Scholarship Symposium*. 4. http://digitalcommons.cedarville.edu/research_scholarship_symposium/2018/podium_presentations/

Kennan, K., & Grantham, D. (1997). The Technique of Orchestration (5th edition). Upper Saddle, NJ: Prentis Hall Publications.

Kirchner, M. J., & Biniecki, S. M. Y. (2019). Student veteran career pathways: A proposed framework for higher education. *New Horizons in Adult Education & Human Resource Development, 31*(2), 27–40. https://doi-org.proxy1.ncu.edu/10.1002/nha3.20248

Landis-Shack, N., Heinz, A. J., & Bonn-Miller, M. O. (2017). Music therapy for posttraumatic stress in adults: A theoretical review. *Psychomusicology: Music, Mind, and Brain, 27*(4), 334–342. https://doi.org/10.1037/pmu0000192

Mayo Clinic. (2022). *Post-traumatic stress disorder* (PTSD): *Diseases and conditions.*
http://www.mayoclinic.org/diseases-conditions/post-traumatic-stress-disorder/symptoms-causes/syc-20355967

Moustakas, C. (1994). Phenomenological research methods. Thousand Oaks, CA: Sage.

Ophir, I., & Jacoby, R. (2020). "Sparks that became a little light over time": A qualitative investigation of musicking as a means of coping in adults with PTSD. *PLoS ONE, 15*(1).
https://doi.org/10.1371/journal.pone.0228050

Osborne, N. J. (2016). From camouflage to classroom: Designing a transition curriculum for new student veterans. *Journal of Postsecondary Education and Disability, 29*(3), 285–292.
https://files.eric.ed.gov/fulltext/EJ1123804.pdf

Ottman, R. W. (2004). Music for Sight Singing (6th edition). Upper Saddle River, NJ: Pearson Prentice Hall.

Pant, U., Frishkopf, M., Park, T., Norris, C. M., & Papathanassoglou, E. (2022). A neurobiological framework for the therapeutic potential of music and sound interventions for post-traumatic stress symptoms in critical illness survivors. *International Journal of Environmental Research and Public Health*, *19*(1331). https://ddoi.org10.3390/ijerph19053113

Peters, V., Bissonnette, J., Nadeau, D., Gauthier-Legare, G., & Noel, M. A. (2023). The impact of musicking on emotion regulation: A systemic review and meta-analysis. *Psychological of Music*, *00*(0), 1-21. DOI: 10.1177/03057356231212362

Stolba, K. M. (1998). The Development of Western Music: A History (3rd edition). Boston, MA: McGraw Hill.

Thomas, R., & Chichaya, T. (2023). A review of literature on the therapeutic use of music with military populations experiencing post-traumatic stress disorder. *Journal of Associated Medical Sciences*, *56*(3), 60-65.

U.S. Department of Veterans Affairs. (2020a). *Annual Benefits Report*, 2020. www.benefits.va.gov/REPORTS/abr/docs/2020_compens ation.pdf

U.S. Department of Veterans Affairs. (2020b). *Annual Benefits Report*, 2020.

www.benefits.va.gov/REPORTS/abr/docs/2020_edu
cation.pdf

U.S. Department of Veterans Affairs. (2020c). *GI Bill
and other education benefit eligibility.*
https://www.benefits.va.gov/education/eligability
Wadsworth, B. K. (2016). Schenkerian Analysis for the
Beginner. *Faculty Publications*, 4126.
https://digitalcommons@kennesaw.edu

Wikipedia contributors. (2024, September 8). Emo. In
Wikipedia, The Free Encyclopedia. Retrieved 04:38,
September 20, 2024, from
https://en.wikipedia.org/w/index.php?title=Emo&old
id=1244725844

Tables and Figures

Table 1:
Song Selections- PTSD- overall

Overall, for PTSD

1. Ambient Instrument-Waterscapes//*Adagio for Strings*, Samuel Barber//432 Hz music, no words//Alternative Rock// "Waterscapes (beach or rainforest)"//*Fire in My Heart*, Two Feet

2. Rock or Alternative//*Appalachian Spring Suit*, Aaron Copeland//Alternative or Heavy Metal, Disturbed//Hip-Hop//Water Life, Whales no seagulls//Friends and Strangers (album), Ronnie Laws

3. Praise and Worship//Soca, specific reggae Bob Marley, steel pan sounds found in Trinidad and Tobago//*Nessun Dorma*, Puccini//Lo-fi/Instrumental//Folk-pop, Noah Kahan or Taylor Swift//*Principles of Lust: Sadness/Finding Love/Sadness (Reprise)*, Enigma

Table 2:
Song Selections- Overall, Hyperawareness

Top 3 selections by PTSD effect

Hyperawareness	
Alternative/Heavy Metal, Disturbed	1. *Alesia*, Eluveitie// 2. *BYOB*, System of a Down// 3. *Chasm*, Flyleaf//

Table 3:
Song Selections- Overall, Depression

Top 3 selections by PTSD effect

Depression	
TN Whiskey, Chris Stapleton; *Take Me Home County Roads*, John Denver; *Oohh Child*, Five Stair Steps//*Adagio for Strings* (Barber), for a good cry, *Here Comes the Sun* (Beatles) to lift my mood//Hip-Hop//432 Hz music//	1. *Bro Hymn*, Pennywise// 2. *How Great Thou Art*// 3. *Morning Has Broken*, John Denver//

Table 4:
Song Selections- Overall, Isolationism

Top 3 selections by PTSD effect

Isolationism	
Wide variety, no Techno or Punk-Rock or Heavy Metal//tend to dive into learning a new guitar piece. Last was *Big Love* by Lindsey Buckingham//Folk-pop, Noah Kahan or Taylor Swift//	1. 2. 3.

Table 5:
Song Selections- Overall, Poor concentration

Top 3 selections by PTSD effect

Poor concentration Trance//432 Hz music//	1. 2. 3.

Table 6:
Song Selections- Overall, Mood swings

Top 3 selections by PTSD effect

Mood swings	
Folk-pop, Noah Kahan or Taylor Swift//	1. 2. 3.

Table 7:
Song Selections- Overall, Anger

Top 3 selections by PTSD effect

Anger	
Variety of Peloton workout Hip-Hop//silence and reflection//432 Hz music//Rock//	1. *Blut Im Auge*, Equilibrium// 2. *Na Na Na*, Chemical Romance// 3. *Zombified*, Falling in Reverse//

Table 8:

Song Selections- Overall, Insomnia

Top 3 selections by PTSD effect

Insomnia	
Waterscapes/Water life, Amazon// Thunderstorm sound generator, hopefully with Alpha waves//432 Hz music//	1. *River Flow in You*, Yiruma// 2. *Autumn*, Antonio Vivaldi// 3. *Tamarack Pines*, George Winston//

Table 9:

Song Selections- Overall, Loss of appetite

Top 3 selections by PTSD effect

Lack of appetite	
	1.
	2.
	3.

Table 10:
Song Selections- Overall, Flashbacks

Top 3 selections by PTSD effect

Flashbacks	
	1.
"I avoid all types of sounds."	2.
//432 Hz music//	3.

Table 11:
Song Selections- Overall, Anxiety

Top 3 selections by PTSD effect

Anxiety	
	1.
"I sing hymns rather than listen to music for acute anxiety."//combines	2.
Hyperawareness and mood swings//country storytelling	3.
songs like *In Color, Come and Get Higher*, and *Remember When*//Lo-fi/ Instrumental//432 Hz music//	

Table 12:
Song Selections- Overall, Memory loss

Top 3 selections by PTSD effect

Memory loss	
	1.
"no music, I keep to myself //432 Hz music//	2.
	3.

Table 13:
Song Selections- Overall, Poor academic success/poor career

Top 3 selections by PTSD effect

Poor academic success/poor career performance	
	1.
	2.
	3.

Table 14

Song Selections- Overall, Fear of crowds

Top 3 selections by PTSD effect

Fear of crowds	1. DMX, almost all songs//
Alternative/Heavy Metal, Disturbed//	2. *I'm Shipping Up to Boston*, Dropkick Murphys//
	3. select Metallica/Beastie Boys//

Table 15:

Song Selections- Other: MusiCorps

Other

MusiCorps:

Y= I, also Guitar for Vets/VA Whole Health Music Therapy.

N= 5

Figure 1:

Demographics - Veterans, by branch of service

Figure 2:

Demographics - Veterans, by branch geographical location

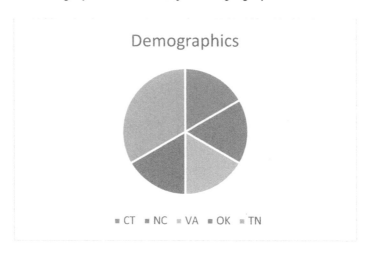

About the Author

 **Dr. Peter Joseph Burke** retired from the US Army in 1996 after serving with the 7th Infantry Division (Light), the 25th Infantry Division (Light), the 10th Mountain Division (Light Infantry), and the US Field Artillery Training Center, Ft. Sill, Oklahoma. He earned his BM in Horn Performance and MA in Teaching from Cameron University. He received his Master of Music Education in Instrumental Conducting from the University of Oklahoma in May 2011. He received his doctorate in education leadership from Northcentral University. At Cameron University, he was an Active Member of the Zeta Tau Chapter of Kappa Kappa Psi from 1997-2001 and served as Vice-President for the 2000-2001 and the 2010-2011 school years and as President from 2011-2012. He performed in numerous performing ensembles, instrumentally and vocally, including the Concert Band, Opera, the CU Jazz Ensemble, and the "Pick-Axe" Band. While at the University of Oklahoma, he performed in the Symphonic Band and the OU Hornsemble and was an Active Member of the Delta Chapter of Kappa Kappa

Psi. He has also served as a conductor of the OU Hornsemble. As a composer, he had two movements of his *Poem for Deanne, which the OU Orchestra read.* In 1996, SGT Burke retired as an Army Bandsman, conductor, and performer. SGT Burke has deployed to Thailand, Korea, Japan, Brunei, the Philippines, Australia, and many others. His notable performances include the funeral for Ellison Onizuka, the Challenger astronaut who died on launch, the Prince of Thailand's birthday, visits from Heads of State, and the New York City Victory Parade after Operation Desert Storm. Mr. Burke has also shared the stage with performers such as Richard Todd, Jonny Highland, Frank Mantooth, Arthur Lipner, the Royal Thailand Army Band, the Band of Her Majesty's Coldstream Guard, and Woody Herman. Dr. Burke is affiliated with ASCAP, Student Veterans of America, and Kappa Kappa Psi. His principal teachers include the United States Army Element School of Music, Dr. Glen Gillis, Dr. William Wakefield, Dr. Joy Nelson, and Dr. Roland Barrett.

Dr. Burke is an independent researcher and publishing author. His published works include *Perceptions of Student-Veterans with PTSD and Availability of Support Services in Academic Life: A Qualitative Descriptive Analysis* and *Discovering Listed PTSD Support on Campus in Higher Education: A Web Survey of Traditional Academic Institutions Home Pages.*

His book, *A Student-veteran's Experience with Higher Education: An Academic Journey*, was released in May 2023. A S-VEwHE: Social, Family, and Fraternal Support... and Peppi, too! is available on Amazon and Kindle.

Peter J. Burke, https://orcid.org/0000-0002-9118-7565

Made in the USA
Middletown, DE
19 January 2025